SEAPORTS

and

PEOPLE *of*

EUROPE

BY

Addie Clark Harding

AS RECOUNTED BY

Garnett Laidlaw Eskew

Eriksson-Taplinger PUBLISHERS NEW YORK

TO THE MEMORY OF

MY GRANDFATHER

ABNER CLARK HARDING

DESIGNER AND LOVER

OF SHIPS

INTRODUCTION

To each and every maritime nation of the world seaports are as vital as merchant fleets and the officers and crews who man them. For where there are no seaports—no docking facilities, no international cooperative shipping and tourist agreements—foreign trade and travel lapse. And where foreign trade and travel languish, the nations of the world are inevitably the worse. This has been true throughout history. It is true today.

In this book, SEAPORTS AND PEOPLE OF EUROPE, Addie Clark Harding of Chicago, a world traveler who has more than once made three long sea voyages in a single year, collaborates once again with Garnett Laidlaw Eskew (an author specializing in marine subjects), and tells the stories of the more important ports of Europe. This volume recounts compactly and readably the stories of the establishment of the sea tracks by early navigators, the founding and romance of each of the seaports that grew up as a result of those early navigators' pioneering.

The book is a real addition to existing maritime literature, for few indeed have been the books devoted exclusively to this subject. Moreover, this is an appropriate time for such a volume. More than at any time in the past, seaports have become the gateways not only of world trade and tourism but for the inflow and outflow of ideas between nations. The more seaports that become gateways, and the more frequently our merchant ships use them, the sooner will that peaceful world, for which we are all striving, evolve and endure.

In an earlier book, AMERICA RIDES THE LINERS, Miss Harding and her collaborator told a lively story of the founding and growth of the American merchant marine and the development of the luxury ocean liner which has accounted for so large a segment of American travel during recent years. This book has had a most stimulating effect upon foreign travel by sea. SEAPORTS AND PEOPLE OF EUROPE should augment that interest.

Miss Harding comes from a long line of seafaring men and shipbuilders. Her genealogy goes straight back, by way of the Sears family of New England, to the famous John Hawkins of London Town,

Queen Elizabeth's great Naval genius, who, among other things, built the ships that defeated the Spanish Armada. Her grandfather and great grandfather were shipbuilders. These facts account in large measure for her continuing travel by sea. One may hope that in succeeding books, other colorful stories of ships and the seas, of which SEAPORTS AND PEOPLE OF EUROPE is a fine example, will be recorded between book covers. We live in a world of interdependent peoples. The more we can learn about each other, the better.

—CLARENCE G. MORSE

CHAIRMAN, FEDERAL MARITIME BOARD;

MARITIME ADMINISTRATOR

U. S. DEPARTMENT OF COMMERCE

PREFACE

Seaports and people . . . people and seaports. Throughout man's recorded history, the two are inseparable. For behind the glamorous
name of every community that has given birth to ships and sailing men—thereby fixing its place in the pages of time—there lies
some tale of romance, some story of courage, some deed of valor
or pathos or humor.

Rogues and dreamers! Connivers and adventurers! Men and
women of vision and enterprise! Individuals who have dedicated themselves to a fixed and unheard-of ideal carried to fruition over formi-
dable opposition! In the chronicles of the ports they built you will find
the story of the family of man.

The creaking wood and slapping sails and the galleys of the
Phoenicians, the Greeks, the Romans and the Carthaginians mark
the early recorded story of man's first attempts to conquer the seas
and to move out beyond the horizons that limited his view of the
world he lived in. In this blue Mediterranean the story of the seaports
thus begins, too. From these early beginnings intrepid sailors, daring
the unknown, pushed out into mysterious and frightening waters to
bring their civilization to Europe's shores.

They started from seaports, and wherever they landed to trade or
explore or make war, they built seaports. So, it is with this time-
hallowed area of mankind's story that this first volume is concerned.
How came the seaports? Why have some prospered while others have
completely disappeared? What were they like in their early days?
What are they like today? What men and women shaped their
destinies?

The search for the answers to these questions leads to a welter of
fact and fantasy. Sometimes truth and myth are so firmly bound together by the unyielding thong of passing years that it is impossible
to tell one from the other. And sometimes the legends reveal more
than the facts.

From the uncharted eastern Mediterranean of thousands of years
ago to Chicago in mid-Twentieth Century may seem to be an illogical
jump. But I have lived in this bustling mid-West metropolis, hard by

erratic Lake Michigan, for more than a quarter of a century. I grew up in an atmosphere of ships and shipbuilding, for my grandfather designed and constructed ships for the lakes trade.

Thus, to me, seaports have always been fascinating places. I have visited forty of them on ocean trips—some several times over. And on each occasion that I enter a foreign port I marvel at the way in which people of many nationalities—often of conflicting national ideologies—meet and mix, cooperate, find mutual interests, transact business side by side where the great ships come in bringing passengers and cargoes and taking away other passengers and other cargoes.

Therefore I rejoice with other Chicagoans that our town is to assume her place among the great ports of the world. Chicago is making ready for the coming of the ships. With the St. Lawrence Seaway she has plans for a combination passenger-freight type ship which will come in out of the sea and make the Windy City its home port. It may be that before too long I can walk down on Michigan Avenue, and from a local steamship office purchase my passage from Chicago to seaports in England, France or elsewhere, boarding the ship right there, without the necessity of making a single change en route!

Now all this incoming and outgoing foreign trade and travel which will follow are bound to have a deepening and broadening influence upon the City—the tone, the outlook, the personality of Chicago and other lake communities.

Here will be located consular offices of more foreign governments than ever before. Trade commissions, purchasing agencies, export and import houses of various nations will open up in Chicago. A larger staff of custom's officers will be needed. One will behold a greater give-and-take between the representatives of these overseas countries and our own—something that will inevitably bring about a better understanding between the people of our country and the nations they represent.

And thus we will see here more of that same friendly spirit and friendly dealing, that improved understanding which one finds in seaports all over the free world.

So, musing here in Chicago which itself is soon to become a world port, I find my mind and heart of their own volition turning to distant seaports to which I know I must return. How often have I ridden ocean liners—large and small—into some foreign port! Each visit has been a discovery, a revelation. The bustle, the shouting, the clatter of many tongues; the greetings of friends and relatives long parted; the swinging of giant cranes moving mountains of baggage and cargo. All these to me are the substance of many happy memories.

As I travel from port to port, it seems to me that the bonds of kinship between people are growing stronger—even in these uncertain times. The stark necessities of survival prod us into it. We need to know, to understand and to trust each other more than ever before.

Every day our own country is widening its associations with other nations, working out cooperative agreements, developing mutually beneficial projects in the fields of science, industry, education, finance, commerce and health. Every year we send more people overseas to represent our interests or to serve other nations. Every year more and more of us spend our holidays in other countries.

The seaports of the world—today, as always—are the gateways through which pass the cargoes of every nation, the peoples and their ideas. Today, they also serve as gateways to better understanding among men.

A.C.H.

Chicago, September 1959

TABLE OF CONTENTS

PART 1

First Pathfinders
at the Entry
of the Sea

LOST in antiquity are the reasons that drew the ancient Phoenicians from their inland settlements to the eastern shores of the Mediterranean.

But whatever the causes for this ancient move, it is known that about 2000 B.C. these astounding people built the first seaport cities known to mankind. From their great ports of Tyre, Sidon and Beirut, they undertook what no men before them had dared. They sailed clean out of sight of land in their small boats, cutting loose entirely from familiar landmarks, gauging their goings and comings by the rising and setting of the sun, the moon and the stars.

Without benefit of chart or compass they established the first sea routes, set up the first trading post in distant lands and conducted history's first recorded give and take of foreign commerce.

Everywhere the Phoenicians went, they left behind them two impressive marks: the quality of their products and the reputation of their abilities as shipbuilders and sailing men.

Sennacherib, King of Assyria; Xerxes, King of Persia; Alexander the Great—these and other powerful monarchs of the time employed the Phoenicians and their ships to do their navigating for them.

Aware that their prosperity depended upon both their ability and their dependability as seamen and merchant-traders, the Phoenicians built up through the years a reputation for commercial integrity and honesty that equalled their demonstrated qualities as navigators.

But they were aware, too, that their prosperity depended equally upon their ability to keep their own great secret. Their methods of navigating and the lines of the routes they established were kept from the knowledge of the contemporary civilizations with which they dealt.

Their textiles and their works of glass and of metal became treasured items throughout the ancient civilized world. When Paris brought his fabulous Helen to the city of Troy, she wore gowns woven by the women of Sidon, which an ancient chronicler has lauded as "bright as the morning sun." A silver bowl with a golden rim was considered by Menelaus to be one of his most prized possessions; it came to him as a gift from the King of Sidon. And the exquisitely wrought pieces of gold, silver and brass that adorned the Temple of Solomon came from Hiram, King of Tyre.

The Hebrews from the time of King Josiah called Tyre "the strong city." In many ways she was to the Phoenicians as Rome is to Italy—the natural center of leadership. Actually, Tyre was a "twin city." Her older section was on the mainland, heavily fortified with massive walls and towers. All traces of that defensive work have disappeared save a few broken arches.

The island of Tyre arose to the status of a first-rate port under King Hiram, the lumber-dealing monarch and friend of David and Solomon of old. On the northern side of the island, a natural, protected harbor provided landing places for both commercial and war fleets. Since this port was not easily accessible in all kinds of weather, another port was built on the south side of the island. It faced Egypt, and since it operated largely under the stimulus of Alexandria, was called the Egyptian port. These two ports of Tyre were connected by a canal—the earliest of inland waterways—making them equally useful in all kinds of weather.

Twenty miles north of Tyre up the coast lay Sidon. It was only a small fishing village like Beth-Saida, inland, on the sea of Galilee—a town often mentioned in the Bible. Its population, however, was an enterprising lot; they made it one of the most successful of Phoenician cities. Like the dwellers at neighboring Tyre, the Sidonians soon rose to fame as seamen. Their pilots sought trade throughout the Mediterranean world. Before the time of Homer their textiles and metals had won fame in other countries and brought to the Sidonians an added wealth.

Foreign commerce in those ancient days was conducted without benefit of currency exchange, customs declarations or even direct contact between buyer and seller. Herodotus describes what he calls the "dumb commerce" of some Phoenicians who had settled at Carthage, bringing with them their seafaring know-how.

They would land on some shore near a town, lay out their wares on the beach and build a huge fire to attract the attention of the townspeople. Then they would withdraw to their ships.

Seeing the blaze, down to the shore would come their clients to examine the goods. If they desired to buy, they would lay out as much gold as they wanted to pay and withdraw to a distance, leaving the goods untouched. Back would come the Carthaginian traders once again to see if the price was right. If acceptable, they would take the money and depart. If not, they would leave the gold where it was, return to their ships and wait for the citizens to make a new offer.

After a few trips back and forth, the bidding would find its level. The merchants would pick up the gold and head out to sea again. The local tribesmen would pick up the merchandise and return to their villages. Everybody would be happy.

This kind of trade spread the culture of the Phoenicians from the ports of Tyre and Sidon as far west as the distant shores of Spain—eventually, indeed, to some of the ports of the North Atlantic. In time the people of the Phoenician cities traveled over to see how the other people lived, and the visits were returned. Here was the origin of travel by sea.

While Phoenician merchants usually brought back only the merchandise and culture of other countries to their own land, there is one

account of a time when they brought back something really special—
Io, daughter of Inachus, King of Argolis, and some of her ladies.

The Phoenicians landed at Argolis, unloading their wares as usual.
Word got around that they had some choice ivory and ebony, ostrich
feathers, embroidered robes as soft as nightfall, gilt mirrors guaranteed
to give back accurately the storied beauty of the Hellenic women.

Io and the ladies of her court simply couldn't wait to get out to
the beach for the sale. They swept down, according to Herodotus, like
a flock of doves upon the merchandise. They could afford to be dove-
like since the rest of the local population had to stand back for the
royal company to do their buying first.

At first the traders looked upon their royal customers only as customers. But Phoenicians were men as well as sailors. Hence it did not
take long for the visiting seamen to come to a romantic though
desperate decision. After a brief period, they suddenly swooped down
upon the unsuspecting customers, even as the customers had swooped
down upon the merchandise. Each man grabbed himself the woman
of his choice and carried her aboard the ship. And it was Ho for
Carthage!

The Phoenicians had a way of founding a little trading post at each
promising point on the shores where they touched. There they would
put up crude warehouses for Phoenician goods. The men who tended
them acted as agents for the home company for both imports and
exports. In the course of time, these little trading posts became
colonies—if indeed they were not already established as such—and
many of them grew to be important seaports.

Among the early voyages of the Phoenicians were several island-
hopping ventures. Centuries before the birth of Christ, they pushed
westward across the Mediterranean to Cyprus. From thence they
struck out for Rhodes and set up a post on that island. Then they
moved on to Crete. From that point on they pushed northward to
trade at Piraeus, seaport for Athens.

One of their early sea routes ran up the long Adriatic Sea to a point
adjacent to the present location of Venice in northeastern Italy.
Another route lay between the island of Sicily and the toe of the big
boot, extending up the western Italian coast to Naples and Ostia, seaport for Rome.

Southwestward from Tyre, the Phoenicians followed a course to what is now Port Said and to Alexandria in Egypt, with a land portage across the Sinai Peninsula to the Gulf of Suez. After that their voyages carried them to what we know today as Benghazi, to Tunis, to Tripoli, and on over to the Iberian Peninsula to trade with Barcelona, Valencia and Cartagena.

Becoming bolder, these intrepid men of the sea pushed out through the Strait of Gibraltar to the port of Lisbon on the Atlantic. Some believe they even visited the southern coast of England and the western coast of France.

Along these ancient routes of the first sea traders stand today some of the ports which they founded. Over the sea-paths which they were the first to travel, came succeeding navigators from other sea-minded nations to establish other new seaports.

The Greeks and the Romans, for instance, came next after the Phoenicians to do more trading and much more colonizing, sometimes adding conquests to their commercial ambition. At first both the Greeks and the Romans followed the routes of their valiant predecessors. But later they sailed up the Adriatic Sea and, sometime early in the Christian era, extended the Phoenicians' sea routes overland across Germany to connect with local trading posts on the North Sea near the present site of Bremen.

Phoenician galleys went pushing up through the island-cluttered Aegean Sea, via the Sea of Azov, to trade with the ports on the Black Sea.

Most important to western civilization today, the Romans sailed on northward up the Atlantic and planted colonies in England, thus sowing the early seeds of England's future sea supremacy.

But when the Phoenicians pushed southward across the Mediterranean to the shores of North Africa, they set the stage for the development of two ports that were to become world famous—Alexandria and Carthage.

There is a circular stone lighthouse on the peninsula at the entrance of Alexandria's harbor. On clear nights you can see it from twenty-five miles out at sea. Near this spot, it is said, the first Ptolemy started construction of the huge lighthouse that became one of the seven wonders of the Ancient World—the mighty Pharos. It proved a boon to early navigators and set the pattern for lighthouses as aids to navigation all over the world.

Alexander the Great founded the city, modestly naming it for himself, more than 300 years B.C. He sized up the site as a fine naval base and laid out plans for it. Then Fate stepped in. Alexander left Egypt—seeking those other worlds to conquer—and never returned to his city save for burial. Cleomenes, his viceroy, took over the first building of Alexandria as an important city.

Next the Romans moved in, about 80 B.C. Thirty-odd years later Julius Caesar came to represent the conquerors.

Although Alexander saw the value of his name city as a seaport, the Egyptians failed for many a long year to take advantage of the conqueror's wisdom. Like Alexander, however, they knew good sailors and good ships when they saw them and, turning to their seafaring neighbors, the Phoenicians, induced them to bring sea trade to their doors—which the Phoenicians were only too glad to do.

The first settlers of Carthage are said to have been refugees from the city of Tyre, led by a beautiful young princess, Elissa, daughter of King Mattan. Princess Elissa, after her father's death, was wooed and won by a wealthy Tyrian nobleman with royal ambitions. But Elissa's brother, Pygmalion, whipped up a revolution denying his sister her royal title and power.

Then Pygmalion killed her husband to prevent further opposition. Grief-stricken, Elissa determined to leave Tyre forever. She would seek a new land and start life all over again. Such an enterprise required money, but since her brother had confiscated the wealth of her husband, Elissa resorted to strategy.

"Permit me to move my goods to the royal palace in Carthage by ship," Elissa pleaded.

Pygmalion agreed, sending along a royal guard to keep an eye on his sister. But before the ships arrived, she had her servants fill several huge bags with sand—the same kind of bags that were used for carrying jewels and other treasures. These her servants carried on board the ship as though they contained all the family jewels and plate. The real treasures meanwhile were smuggled aboard ship and hidden during the loading.

Once out at sea, Elissa proclaimed her desire to make a sacrifice to the spirit of her departed husband and commanded the sailors to throw overboard the bags of sand. Before her brother's officers could stop them, the sailors jettisoned what appeared to be rich treasures.

"When my brother hears of this," Elissa then announced, "you will probably lose your heads for being derelict in your duties. Let me advise you, my friends, that you will remain healthy much longer if you sail at once for some distant shore far beyond the reach of my brother's revenge. I am offering you the choice . . ."

Pygmalion's men chose Carthage!

There is another appealing incident in this time-honored legend. When the band of refugees from Tyre landed at the site of Carthage, they first bargained with the local tribesmen for land. The tribesmen tried to drive a hard bargain, offering to sell a piece of land equal to the area that could be encompassed by an ox hide.

Elissa, not one to be taken in by a country slicker, agreed to the deal with a straight face and paid down the price in jewels. Then, after a little knife-work on an oxhide, she began to mark off the first survey of the boundaries of the historical city of Carthage. The hide had been cut into narrow strips and tied together to make a long rope. It covered a rather sizeable piece of land.

Elissa is better known to us as Dido. Her Carthage began to prosper so well that she received an offer of marriage from King Irabus of Lybia, from whose people she had bought her land. But Dido couldn't abide Irabus. Spurned, the King threatened war. In desperation, Dido is said to have solved the dilemma by burning herself to a crisp on a funeral pyre. If this seems a rather unimaginative way to evade a suitor, at least, it saved the city from war.

The poet Vergil was not satisfied with this sort of unhappy ending, so he made up another, only slightly less attractive. In the *Aeneid*, he has Dido visited by Aeneas, hero of Troy. They fall in love, but Aeneas receives a message, supposedly from Jove, advising him that this is not the girl for him. When he leaves, poor Dido takes to her funeral pyre again.

The English composer, Henry Purcell, wrote his own version of the story in the opera "Dido and Aeneas." Although he converted Aeneas into a handsome sailor, like the other, he left Dido once again to a fiery death.

The original plot of ground bought by Elissa topped a hill rising about two hundred feet above the sea. Below, in the Gulf of Carthage, lie the remains of the harbor today. There were two harbors, in fact— one for commercial trade, the other for the home defense fleet. The commercial piers were served by a man-made lagoon of about sixty acres. You reached the naval base, beyond the commercial piers, by a canal. It was a giant circle of moorings, with a tiny island in the center where the presiding admiral could review his fleet.

It was Hannibal who brought Carthage her greatest fame. His military genius became the wonder of the world and his campaigns in Africa, Spain and Italy are still read by military students. But in the second Punic War, as he was set to drive into the heart of Italy and subdue forever the nemesis of his beloved city, he met the fate of many a brilliant leader. While the road to Rome stood open before him, the Carthaginian Senate was having a spasm of economy.

At home, in the quiet of their chambers, far from the battle front, they just couldn't agree to the need for raising more funds to support another campaign by Hannibal. They dallied away his advantage. With their hesitation the attack on Rome was stalled; perhaps the entire course of history changed.

But despite Hannibal's military genius and in spite of Dido's penchant for fiery suicide, Carthage suffered a rough fate. It was captured and destroyed, rebuilt, wiped out by epidemic, resettled and recaptured. Finally, in 698 A.D., Carthage disappeared from the scene for good, the victim of a massive Arab invasion.

While Sidon, Tyre and Carthage have had their historians, what of such romantically named ports as Caesarea, Myra, Hadrumetum, Utica, Puteoli? Once flourishing and important seaports, today they are either obscure fishing villages or merely hallowed names of cities long since gone—victims of the forward push of Time.

Yet each had its brief flash of glory, the result of some historic personality or world shaking event.

Jesus once visited Caesarea, and it was St. Paul's point of departure on his great trip to Rome. Taken and retaken, it was finally burned by the Syrians in the Tenth Century. Today, it is a small village, where only a few broken columns, parts of a fortress and an aqueduct remain to mark the glories of the past.

The great trading center of ancient Lycia (today's Turkey) was Myra. It was here that Paul changed ships on his first voyage to Rome.

Today, one can find only the remnants of a granary, inscribed with the name of Hadrian, Roman Emperor.

On the eastern coast of Tunisia lies the sleepy coastal town of Susa. Nothing in its present appearance can make it believable that it once bore the fine name of Hadrumetum, that Hannibal used it as a base of operations, that it was taken by Caesar and that the Roman emperor Trajan later made it into a colony that flourished for its brief period. Yet, such are the glorious facts.

Fifteen miles north of Carthage lay Utica, one of the first North African ports noted by historians. Cato fell back upon it to make his last stand against Caesar. For hundreds and hundreds of years nothing marked the old site of this proud city but salt marshes. But excavations finally uncovered an amphitheatre with a capacity of some 2000 spectators—proof that the area was once the center of daily life for a people who, among other things, enjoyed their pleasures.

Puteoli, the greatest commercial port of the ancient Italian peninsula, played a brief but major role in the development of western civilization. One of the most stirring accounts of a sea voyage ever written is that which Luke penned to describe St. Paul's voyage to Rome. Here are its concluding dramatic words:

And after three months we set sail in a ship of Alexandria, which had wintered in the island, whose sign was THE TWIN BROTHERS. *And touching at Syracuse, we tarried there three days. And from thence, by tacking, we arrived at Rhegium. And after one day a south wind sprang up, and on the second day we came to Puteoli: where, finding brethren, we were consoled among them, remaining seven days; and thereupon we came to Rome.*

And so this now obscure seaport in the Bay of Naples had its very brief, but glorious moment in the spotlight of world history.

PART 2

Ports and People
Around the Boot

NAPLES:
Port of Romance and Intrigue

I T IS a far cry from St. Paul to a regal and proud daughter of Maria Theresa, Empress of Austria.

But these two divergent historic figures are in fact bound together by the endlessly lapping waves of the blue Bay of Naples. For the same natural advantages that motivated the ancients to establish a seaport at Puteoli—the ample natural harbor, the proximity to major trade routes, the protection afforded by surrounding mountains—led over the centuries to the development of Naples as a major port.

Maria-Carolina, daughter of the indomitable Empress, was not only a Queen—she was a woman. She gambled her life to avenge the death of a royal sister; she and her lover helped free Naples from French domination, and together they launched Naples on its great career.

The story of the Port of Naples began when the Greeks became interested in the fishing villages on the Italian shore and entered the exquisite blue bay at the foot of Vesuvius, several centuries before the birth of Christ. Capaccio, the Italian mapmaker, admitted that "the Greeks were masters in building cities in the best locations."

14

An early panorama of Naples from the Bay.

Greek culture was so firmly established in Naples in 300 B.C. that the Romans, when they'd captured the city, traveled there by the hundreds to improve their minds, their manners and social standing. It was the smart and fashionable thing to do in those days. In fact, the Emperor Nero chose Naples as the center of culture in which to make his debut as a singer.

Along with Maria-Carolina, several other women made Neapolitan history. First among them was Pharenthope, the siren who sang with such haunting beauty, according to Homer himself, that she and her sisters lured sailors and ships—Lorelei fashion—to their destruction. Then there was Joanna I, early Queen of the little city-state of Naples. Joanna was all woman. Naples remembers her for her feminine passion for beautiful clothes and jewelry and for fine living and court pageantry.

In 1768 Maria-Carolina was married off by proxy, in Venice, to King Ferdinand of Naples, son of Charles of Spain. The bride was only sixteen, the King, seventeen.

She came riding into town, a bride clad in a "gown of turquoise blue with gold braiding." She recorded in her diary, "I am convinced that I am all dressed up to be a political sacrifice." Then she saw the King for the first time, and she was sure of it. He was scrawny. He had a big nose; people had nicknamed him *Nasone*, which means just that.

"He is very ugly," the young Queen wrote in disgust to a friend, "but one gets used to that . . . What irritates me most is that he thinks himself handsome and charming . . . He says he loves me uncommonly, but does not a thing I want done." It was, of course, purely a political alliance.

For all that, the young Queen seems not to have been too dismayed by her husband's lack of charm. Over the years she bore him eighteen children, managed a kingdom, and became a person of considerable influence on the continent of her time.

She owed much to her mother, the ambitious and iron-willed Maria Theresa, who got her off to a running start. The old Empress gave each of her daughters a sound education in the fine art of government. She saw to it that their marriage alliances gave them ample legal protection. When drawing up the marriage contract for Maria-Carolina, mama insisted on a provision that her daughter sit in the State Council from the day she bore her first son.

Being a dutiful daughter, Maria-Carolina complied—producing her son soon enough. From that day she not only sat in the Council of State, she also managed the whole Kingdom. The King had his hands full with his hunting and his other pleasurable pursuits. The details of government bored him.

In Naples, they speak of Maria-Carolina as the "Goddess of our Port," for it was she who first came to understand the city's importance in the world-maritime picture.

The Neapolitan Navy—both military and merchant—was in a sad state of disrepair. Maria-Carolina soon remedied that. With her brother, the Grand Duke of Tuscany, she began to look about for someone who could help her develop suitable ships and berths for them to dock at. It is right here that romance enters the picture, in the person of an adventurous young Englishman—John Acton—who had distinguished himself as a designer of ships, a naval engineer and a strategist.

Acton, a sailor-soldier of fortune, was forty-two years old, and a bachelor. While it is said he was not handsome, he had a commanding personality, a penetrating gaze, a slim, agile figure—qualities that most certainly a lonely young Queen would appreciate.

At first jealousy sat heavy upon the brow of King Ferdinand. Acton, fifteen years older than the King, had so much that the monarch lacked. He was far more experienced in the affairs of state, a man of the world who knew much about romance.

Wisely, Acton refused to live at the Royal Palace, settling himself instead at Castellamare, near the docks. But the lovely young Queen, an expert in all the little arts of coquetry, kept her eye on him. Either Acton was not an accomplished actor, or he didn't cross enough palms with silver. Anyhow, King Ferdinand soon got wind of what was happening and threatened to kill both the Queen and Britisher if he ever discovered them together again.

Realist that he was, however, Ferdinand knew that Acton was indispensable to the creation of the kind of seaport Naples must have. A port, that is, which would enable Naples to become a really independent kingdom and thus enable her to build up her shipping to a point where she could compete with other European fleets. Thus Carolina was accomplishing two things in retaining Acton: she was pleasing her people because of the quality of Acton's work and she was appeasing her own loneliness for love. By her persuasive powers she overcame the objections of certain jealous members of the Court. Acton remained.

King Ferdinand finally saw Acton's carefully drawn plan for completely reorganizing the Neapolitan marine in January of 1779. We can well imagine it was a grudging respect the King gave the Englishman—but it is to be said to his credit that he gave it. Ferdinand even went so far as to refuse to comply with the demands of the great Napoleon that Acton be banished from the city. Bonaparte was fearful—and rightly so—of the influence of such a Britisher at the Court of Ferdinand.

Doggedly, Acton kept at his work—no doubt with occasional time out for a visit with the Queen. He modernized the shipyards at Castellamare until they could stack up well with those of Venice, then the best in all Italy. For each of the next six years, Acton launched for Naples a ship of the line plus a lot of gun-boats, frigates and merchant ships. At last Naples had become a first-rate sea power, her war-fleet

17

alone numbering 150 sail. And the merchant marine all this time kept pace with the fighting fleet.

Following Acton's achievements Naples' sea trade revived: with Genoa, with Russia, with Greece, with other nearby maritime countries. Those tubby little pollocks built at the yards of Naples' neighbor, Sorrento, sailed regularly to France, Portugal, Spain, England; some of them ventured over to the newly created United Colonies of America. The world began to look upon Naples as a great maritime power.

From the beginning of the year 1793 the Queen had been deeply worried about her younger sister Marie Antoinette, Queen of France. As time proved, she had good reason for her anxiety, for it was in August of that same year that news reached her that her sister had died under the guillotine. Maria-Carolina was devastated. Her bitter anger arose, and under the portrait of her dead sister she wrote:

"I shall pursue my vengeance until the tomb!"

Five years later, her opportunity arose. In June, 1798, the British Naval hero, Lord Nelson, sailed into Naples harbor with a fleet of war ships, and dropped anchor. Nelson was in hot pursuit of the French fleet, although thus far it had eluded him. France was reported to be on the eve of launching an expedition to India and Nelson was under Admiralty orders to hunt down the French ships involved and sink them.

Nelson's fleet, however, had taken on no water or food since May. Without fresh supplies, his chase must end. Although he knew very well that any appeal to King Ferdinand would bring no results, he nevertheless tried. The French had forced the King of Naples to sign an agreement that he would permit no more than two British warships to land at any one time in the Harbor of Naples, and the French Resident for the Revolutionary Government kept an eagle eye upon every ship in port.

"I'd like to help you in every way possible," Ferdinand told Nelson, in effect, "but I don't dare. The French would strike us with brutal reprisal. Perhaps we'd even see *la guillotine* set up in the streets of Naples!"

But day and night Maria-Carolina had been racking her mind for some way to help this little British Admiral and thus be avenged on France for her sister's death.

Now, finally, the idea came. If her scheme were discovered, well she knew the French would come down upon Naples like Sennacherib upon the Hebrew host. She might even receive the same fate as her sister, paying with her head the price of her devotion. But—if Nelson beat the French! Ah then, she might liberate her own dear Naples from the despised Gallic domination.

So the Queen gambled. She sent a note to Nelson, ordering him and his ships out of the harbor, as per French orders. But a secret note accompanying that order directed the Governor of the ancient port of Syracuse on the Ionian Sea to give all possible aid to the British admiral.

The Queen's gamble paid off. Nelson victualed his ships, caught up with the French fleet at Alexandria, demolished it. Maria-Carolina felt that Marie Antoinette had been avenged.

Under the picture of her dead sister she wrote another line, "*Je Vous Avenge!*"

Those shipyards at Castellamare, "modernized" in the eighteenth century by John Acton, were laid waste by the bombings of World War II. But they have been remodernized, and Naples now has three major yards capable of taking on 20,000–ton ships for repairs. Her docks have modern loading equipment and capacious warehouses, while railroad and truck terminals speed the transfer of import and export. A rapidly-developing industry on the nearby Island of Sicily has added enormously to Naples' port business. Sicily's increasing importance as a new center of manufacturing has drawn industrial capital from many nations—much of it from the United States. Naples with her superior harbor facilities is the nearest great port to the new Sicilian activity.

Liners and freighters arrive in the Port of Naples each day, bringing passengers and cargoes from all nations. In one recent year, there were more than 5,000 ship arrivals and departures. Nearly half a million tons of cargo cleared from Naples for the United States alone. We import more table wines from Italy than from any other country—wines with names such as Valpolicella, Bardolino, Soave. Three and a half million gallons of Italian wines came over in one year—the major part of it through the Port of Naples.

And Naples' ability to handle this considerable tunnage might never have developed had it not been for Queen Maria-Carolina and her Englishman, John Acton.

VENICE:
Beauty on a Sea Trade Foundation

I N THE days that recorded Maria-Carolina's attempts to salvage both her personal life and the prosperity of her Neapolitan kingdom, the leading seaport of the Italian peninsula was Venice.

The Queen City of the Adriatic, with its 120 islands, reminds one of the traditional story of the three blind men and the elephant. Having each felt a different part of the beast's anatomy, the three men gave completely different descriptions of what an elephant looks like, basing their concepts on their explorations of his trunk, his legs and his tail, respectively.

Venice is like that. It is many different things to many different people. Its visitors carry away widely differing impressions of what feature best represents this fabulous city:

An early view of Venice from the Sea.

"St. Mark's Cathedral," one will tell you.
"Piazza di San Marco," another will answer.
"The Doge's Palace by all means," opines a third.

Others, especially romantic young girls, will say that Venice's *pièce de résistance* is a gondola ride on the Grand Canal and all that it entails, while to the serious art lover, Venice is paintings by Tintoretto, Titian, Vecchio, Tiepolo, and many other great artists.

In truth, the city has the various facets of some well-cut gem. Turn it whichever way you please, beauty shines back at you.

But Venice's architectural and artistic beauty rests upon a solid commercial foundation. It would have been impossible to concentrate in this one city so much solid and enduring beauty but for the yielded wealth of her rich seaport and the flourishing foreign trade that dates back to her golden era, in the time of the City-States.

The strategic position of Venice had for centuries much to do with the commercial power she held over the Mediterranean. Down from southern Germany through the Brenner and Gottherd passes came traders bringing textiles, leather, furs, metal and twine. By sea the Venetian galleys carried out cargoes of spices, dyes, paper, alum, weapons bound for Bruges, Antwerp and German ports. These they traded for fish, wax, grain, wool, tallow, tin and lead.

The story of Venice, too, is the story of one early commanding personality. The spirit of the astute leadership of one of her Doges lives strong in her memory. Under the policy making of Henrico Dandolo, Venice rose to the peak of her glory in the thirteenth century with the capture of Constantinople. This gave her complete domination of the sea trade both of the East and the North.

Dandolo was an old man then—in 1192—and blind! But despite his eighty-four years and his physical handicap he saw far into the future and dreamed great dreams for his city. "Blind old Dandolo!" they called him, but it was an affectionate nickname. Some say he was blinded in battle; others that he was the victim of torture by the Greek Emperor when Dandolo served as Venetian Ambassador at the Court of Constantinople.

Dandolo possessed a da Vinci versatility. He turned his abilities to many endeavors successfully: admiral, diplomat, military leader and patriot. He reigned less than fourteen years, but his sagacity, his sense of justice and his brilliance as a strategist won him undying fame. During his reign his beloved city rose high and waxed strong.

"Oh, for one hour of blind old Dandolo!" lamented Lord Byron in *Childe Harold's Pilgrimage.*

Pope Innocent III called upon all Christendom in 1198 to organize a fourth Crusade, invade the Holy Land "and deliver the Holy Sepulcher from the hands of the Infidels." In France, a priest, Father Fulk of Neuilly, pleaded the Pope's case and did such a good job that the French nobles gathered an army and sent ambassadors to Venice to enlist aid to furnish sea transport to Constantinople. Venice had the ships. Venice had the port. And Venetians numbered among their population the finest seafaring men in the world.

Although the old Doge was a devout man, he retained a practical head on his shoulders. He had to remember, he told the Frenchmen, that he was the leader of a city which made its living from the sea. He could not venture her ships, her sailors, her money without some assurance of adequate return. After some negotiations, Dandolo finally agreed to transport the Crusaders to Palestine for a fee of 85,000 marks, plus half of "the spoils of the Crusade." The latter was to include all that was taken both in goods brought home and lands captured and occupied.

Since any proposal of the Doge had to be ratified by the people, Dandolo called the populace together in the Basilica of the Cathedral of San Marco for a most memorable meeting. On what has been described as "a gentle day in the winter of the year 1201," the High Altar was prepared for the solemnities of High Mass. Old Dandolo, resplendent in a cape and a cloak of gold, led the six French ambassadors before the gathered crowd.

Outside, in the piazza, surged the assembled citizens, brown and wrinkled seafaring men, artisans, shopkeepers, peddlers, gentlemen of fortune, dandies, women and children. After mass, Dandolo mounted the high pulpit and called upon the French to present their petition. One of the noblemen, Godfrey de Villehardouin, stepped up and spoke. His words are still of record:

"Messieurs," he pleaded, "the noblest and most powerful barons of France have sent us to you to pray you to have pity upon Jerusalem in bondage to the Turk, and for the love of God to accompany us to avenge the shame of Christ; and knowing that no nation is so powerful upon the seas as you, they have charged us to implore your aid and not to rise from our knees till you have consented to have pity upon the Holy Land." The ambassadors then actually fell upon their knees in supplication before the crowd.

The voice of old Dandolo rang out clear and strong in the vast church: "You are allied with the bravest of living men," he told the people, "for the greatest purpose which man can embrace. I am old and weak and my body has great need of rest, yet I clearly see that no one can lead you to this enterprise with the authority which is mine as chief of the Republic. I pray you, give me leave to take the cross that I may lead you and watch over you, and let my son take my place here to guard the territories of Venice while I go forth to live or die with you and with these pilgrims."

As Villehardouin recounts the story, the French wept at the eloquence of the old man. And the people of Venice cried out with one voice, "We grant it! We grant it!"

By September of the next year, 1202, the Venetian galleys were surging against their warps in the Canal of Giudecca. A fleet of three hundred sails—fifty galleys, two hundred and fifty other ships. Three great vessels led the fleet, the *Aquila*, the *Paradiso*, and the *Pellegrina*. The standard of the Republic, bearing the Lion of St. Mark, floated from the mastheads of the great ships. The flags of the other nations taking part in the Crusade flew below and at the yard-arms.

Historians point out that the idealistic purposes of the Crusades often seemed to get lost among the mercantile interests involved. As if in support of this accusation, Dandolo's fleet made a stop in the first few days on its Holy Mission to capture the nearby city of Zara. The political and plundering detour brought down upon the expedition the wrath of Pope Innocent. Yet for all that, the splendor of Henrico Dandolo has not been dimmed by disparagement of the real nature of his motivation. His capacity to inspire respect in the men of every nation who took part in the enterprise remains a legend.

Many months later, after profitable "visits" to several ports along the Mediterranean, the flotilla arrived before the walled city of Constantinople. The crusaders were dismayed by the enormous fortification, consisting of several thick walls, one within the other, the whole topped by 400 towers.

Had they known that their little army of 40,000 men was outnumbered ten to one by the defenders beyond those walls they would have been even more intimidated. But dauntless old Dandolo inspired them, struck fire in their hearts. Accounts of the capture of Constantinople are legion. One of the most graphic is that recorded by the great historian, Edward Gibbon:

The Venetians, led by aged Dandolo, rowed their ships to the foot of the towers that came down to the sea. Dandolo's ship led the way. In complete armour he stood in the prow, the standard of St. Mark beside him. When his ship touched the foot of the walls, he was the first to set foot upon the ramparts of the infidels. Scaling ladders were lifted all about him. The agile Venetians scrambled up the walls. A steady hail of arrows whistled over their heads from thousands of archers

Another view of Venice.

"War Machines" on the decks hurled ammunition at the walls. Within a short time twenty-five towers fell to the invaders, assuring the fall of Constantinople.

Dandolo never lived to return to his beloved Venice. Early in June, 1205, he died, leaving behind him the lasting memory of a great patrician, a man of tact, of courage, integrity and leadership.

Above one of the doors of the Church of San Marco there are today four great bronze horses. These were a gift from the spoils of the fourth religious Crusade that sailed out of the Port of Venice under the beloved, blind leader Dandolo.

Off the Grand Canal, near the Campanile—that seagazing tower

25

more than three hundred feet high—stand two massive stone columns, one red, the other gray. Those two columns came from the Holy Land in the year 1127—religious relics to adorn the city of watery streets. They lay flat on the quay for several years because no contractor would undertake the task of raising heavy stone shafts of such massiveness.

Finally the current Doge offered a reward to anyone who would undertake it, whereupon one Nicola Barattiere, late of Lombardy, volunteered.

Down into the muddy Venetian shore he drove long piles for a foundation. Then with the aid of ropes and some crude ship capstans he hoisted the columns into place. Deeply impressed, the Doge watched the performance.

"Fine!" said the Doge. "What do you want for a reward?"

"Give to me and my descendants," Nicola answered modestly, "as long as we live in Venice, the right to set up and operate gambling tables between these two columns!"

Although public gambling was against the law of Venice, the Doge winked at this minor infraction and gave Nicola what he asked. The successful contractor set up his tables right there near the wharf, between the two columns. But the Doge quickly designated the spot between the two columns as the place of public execution, believing this would invest the spot with a pall of misfortune so that no one would come there to gamble.

Nevertheless, Nick and his descendants grew rich and powerful through the concession of the columns. Sea captains, sailormen, wharf men, dandies from the Rialto, gentlemen of serious affairs and possibly some ladies all came to Nick's table to woo the goddess of chance. Sometimes they were lucky, but Nick & Co. came off winners in the end.

To this day in Venice you will hear down along the water front the name Barattiere used as a synonym for a money-changer, a usurer, a dishonest gambler.

Venice, in her prime, traded with every known nation that had seaports from which to trade. The city had so great a problem with her transient population (tourists, we would call them today) that she had to build two hotels to accommodate them—the *Moon Hotel* and the *White Lion Hotel*. They became known far and wide and set the pattern for later hostelries.

In the shipbuilding field also Venice became world-renowned. She made a science of ship construction even in those crude times, and every day of the year one heard the whang of mallets and hammers and the shouts of workmen in her busy shipyards. The smell of shavings and sawdust permeated the air of the seaside.

Venice developed two major types of vessels, the long ship propelled by galley oars, and the "round" ship with great spreads of sail. The galleys themselves were of two types. One was light, swift and easily maneuverable, designed to escort and protect convoys of merchant ships from the pirates who infested the seas in those days, as well as from ships of enemy nations. The other galley-type, larger and designed for trading voyages with cargoes, was also very fast. Historians say that the big galleys of Venice offered the surest maritime means of transport available during two entire centuries.

These big merchantmen galleys of Venice carried crews of more than two hundred. Every man on board had to be a competent oarsman, a skilled sailor and a first-rate fighting man. Each ship carried twenty bowmen (or, after 1486 when the use of gun powder became prevalent, a detachment of gunners) all of whom were selected by public contest from among the best shots in Venice.

The cost of operating ships so manned ran high, of course—but so did freight rates. The owners charged enough to warrant an ample profit for themselves and seem to have had no trouble in getting what they asked. Old records in Venice show that one fleet alone brought in two and a half million pounds of spices from Alexandria every winter over a long period of years. Crewmen of the galleys achieved a high reputation. They were cocks of the walk in the Port of Venice and were given special privileges by the city.

As an added inducement, the crewmen were allowed to do a little trading of their own on the side. Each member of the crew was assigned a small cargo space in which he could stow some merchandise of his own to sell in foreign ports at enormous profits. But with the development of the full-rigged ships and naval artillery, the galleys as a type were doomed. Open-deck as they were, galleys were peculiarly susceptible to artillery fire.

The "round" ships of Venice are the forebears of the famous sailing ships of the line that made possible the conquest of the open seas. At first the clumsy little tubs had only a single mast. Then some

Venice, c. 1571.

wise shipbuilder added another mast and more canvas. Along came another captain and added still another mast.

When the square-rigged ships came from the north, brought down to the Mediterranean by Basque pirates of Bayonne, the Venetian shipbuilders adapted the rig to their own uses. From these early combinations of types the "full-rigged ship" of the heyday of sail evolved. They had, even from the first, greater cargo space than the galleys. They could be operated by a smaller crew which meant that freight rates could be reduced. Shipping of bulk cargoes now became a profitable business.

Not only were high priced cargoes—spices, silks, furs and handicrafts —carried, but the ships began to take cotton and alum from Syria

and wine from Crete. Other seaports sent out oil, grain, wood, and stone—all inbound to the Port of Venice. Thus the funny little "round" ships, once scorned by the lusty crews of the proud and swift galleys, metamorphosed into beautiful Queens of commerce.

But as the first of these new ships slipped down the ways into the blue waters of the Adriatic, she carried away with her the fortunes of Venice. For, with the bigger, faster ships, the captains of other City-States began to roam far abroad to bring back cargoes and plunder. The Adriatic became a dead-end sea alley. The great ships that were the pride of all Venice in time delivered her power into the hands of her rivals, and the glories of the days of Henrico Dandolo were forever lost to history.

GENOA:
Strictly Business

G ENOA is the gateway to the teeming industries of northern Italy. Although a greater total number of ships enters the ports of Venice and Trieste, Genoa clears in a year more tonnage of vessels and goods than any other Italian port. Genoa has always been seaminded —a great colonizer.

The port's history can be traced back to a time well before the founding of Rome. Until the second Punic War, Genoa was thriving on her sea trade and doing very well. Then the Carthaginian Naval Commander Mago brought his fleet of crude ships into the Bay of

Panorama of Genoa.

Genoa and took the city by storm. Mago's sailors set upon the people, destroyed many buildings and carried off many of the ladies in the barbaric manner of those early times.

Following the Carthaginians came the Romans, and after the Romans, the Franks. With the downfall of the Empire of Charlemagne the people of Genoa pulled themselves together, took an oath of mutual defense, organized their own little independent republic and declared themselves autonomous. Genoa wanted only peace and commerce.

At once she turned her eyes to the sea, with no desire whatever for conquest but with pronounced commercial intent. Soon Genoese ships were ranging far and wide in the Mediterranean, bearing adventurous citizens to establish new trade outposts. Some went as far as the shores of the Black Sea where new settlements sprang up—villages that served the same purpose as the pioneer outposts developed in our own country centuries later.

Typical of the pioneer Genoese merchants who profited by this expansion was Armano the Skinner (the reference being not to any dishonest dealings on his part, but to his "profession"; he was in the fur business.)

Armano went out to sea to get the business before it came to the Port of Genoa. He set up his business at the lonely outpost town of Bonifacio on the strait between Corsica and Sardinia, the beginning of the thirteenth century.

Natives in that rugged countryside produced only two products—skins and cheese. But Armano knew that Bonifacio was on the busiest of trade routes in the Mediterranean. Ships carrying cargo from Liguria to Africa, and from other ports to the Levant, found it a good place to stop. The harbor on the Strait also offered a fine location for pirates who liked to pick up a fat cargo now and then.

Armano did a whopping agent's business in such things as cloth from France and Flanders, spices from the Orient, grain and silver from other ports—and skins which originated right where he had stationed himself. The inventory in his will of his worldly goods listed "364 skins of she-goats; 280 lambskins; sixty-three tanned hides; thirty-four deer skins; twenty kid skins; three fox skins and two marten skins" among other things.

To his wife, Orenga, and his daughter, Riccafina, he left five houses, an orchard, shares in several ships and a thriving business. Armano was a type that was becoming increasingly prevalent in Genoa.

For centuries during ancient and medieval times Genoa remained a major power in the Mediterranean, with her far-flung Colonial Empire. But increased wealth for the city carried with it the seeds of her own destruction.

But in time arose the so-called Bank of Genoa—really an organization of worthy citizens connected with the Cathedral of Genoa. Those were the days when the Church played a major role in government.

By both Church and State, the Bank was given the right to engage the military forces of the Republic in conflict.

Bank members had enterprise and imagination. As they sat in their great picturesque villas above the Bay, they surveyed the ships at anchor below them, thinking of the settlements they had helped to establish, like those in the Balearic Islands off Spain's coast. It occurred to them that the fortunes of the Republic of Genoa and of themselves could be greatly enriched by further plunder of the Spanish towns.

So, in a spirit of patriotism, mixed with considerable regard for their own fortunes, the Bank members advanced the funds for the launching of new expeditions of conquest. As a hedge against the many hazards of war, the bankers set the proviso that they would be repaid regardless of the outcome—win, lose or draw. There was another condition: the bankers were to be given first priority to bid on all the loot brought back from the expedition, and on the lands that were captured by the Genoese invaders!

When the first fleets prepared to sail, Genoa became a beehive of industry. Streets crowded with sailors and soldiers preparing for departure! Shops doing a land-office business day and night! Docks swarmed with ship's carpenters, sailmakers, caulkers and other craftsmen of the maritime profession engaged in outfitting a fleet!

News reached the Genoese in 1136 that their 155 ships and sixty galleys had landed at Almerice, in Spain, and had taken the city with, as an earlier historian puts it, "great slaughter and vast booty." A year later the thriving community of Tortoso met the same fate.

When the conquering heroes returned to be met by a joyous throng gathered to greet them, they brought cargoes of inestimable value. Sailors carried the booty ashore and spread it out for all to see. Genoese merchants gathered close, casting their shrewd appraising eyes over the treasures from Spain—exquisite silks, rich tapestries and brocades, silver and gold plate, jewels of every variety. But then, the city officials stepped up and made a devastating announcement:

"No bids can be made until the Bankers have been given a chance to select what they want in payment for underwriting the conquest."

Most of the lucrative trade of the port fell straight into the laps of the Bank members. "Anybody who wants to buy captured loot or land, let him come to us," they said.

Soon the Bank of Genoa began to take on added responsibilities, added powers. With most of the citizenry indebted to it, its members received the power "to prescribe public laws, civil or criminal; to establish courts and appoint judges; to issue passports." And finally "to invoke the power of Ecclesiastical excommunication against all refractory debtors to the Bank, clergymen as well as laymen."

What had actually happened was that the gallant little Republic of Genoa had been absorbed by the Bank. And from that day she began to lose her stature as a colonial and sea power in the Mediterranean.

But although the City-State lost its colonies, through the centuries Genoa has remained a major port of vast importance. American ships began to trade with Genoa and other Italian ports shortly after our independence had been won. Before steam came along, American sailing packets from New York and New England, long before the days of the clipper ships, sought the docks of Italian cities with profit to the merchants and shipping and to the City-States on the Big Boot.

Two of the many reasons why Genoa has become the chief port in modern Italy have a special importance to both the development of world trade and better understanding among nations.

First, Genoa is one of the key seaports in the international association called the European Common Market whose member nations are Belgium, Netherlands, France, West Germany, Italy and Luxembourg. They have agreed to eliminate trade barriers between themselves and facilitate commerce with other nations.

Second, Genoa's modern efficient port facilities provide great inducements to industrial capital from other nations. And Genoa still builds great ships, too. Her shipyards turn out modern ocean liners one after another. In 1956, the Ansaldo yards delivered the 21,250-ton *Gripsholm* to the Swedish-American Line. The same year the 52,000-ton super-tanker *Agrigentum* slid down the same ways. A great luxury liner, *Leonardo da Vinci*, will soon take the water to replace the lost and lovely *Andrea Doria*, in the North Atlantic fleet of the Italian Line.

Genoa has persistent recuperative powers. Like other major cities of Italy she suffered devastating destruction in her shipping facilities during World War II. But today she has been rebuilt into one of the

The Port of Genoa in Columbus' time.

best equipped and busiest seaports in all of Europe. She boasts twenty big cargo piers and quays stretching fifteen miles up and down her waterfront, providing berthing for more than 200 ships simultaneously. Loading and unloading operations can be carried on simultaneously by 100 ships.

With her two million square feet of warehousing and transit sheds, her more than eighty plants and shops to take care of fitting-out and repair jobs, Genoa ranks alongside the largest ports of Europe.

Thus, the history of seaport Genoa has been a consistently told tale of "strictly business." The few names that cling to her historic past are those of shrewd and far seeing merchants like Armano the Skinner, rather than those of romantic explorers, swashbuckling adventurers or beautiful Queens.

Yet, there is one name of a claimed native son that resounds through those pages that record man's achievements—a name of whose bearer Genoa is sufficiently proud to have erected a statue, which to-day commands a position overlooking the busy modern harbor. Unfortunately, the Genoese of his time were a little too busy with their commercial interests to pay much attention to him and his radical idea. And so they let him escape westward to the Iberian peninsula, whence he sailed one day on one of history's grandest voyages.

His name? Cristoforo Columbo.

PART 3

Ports and People of Iberia

SPAIN:
The Story of Two Expatriates

THAT Christopher Columbus was actually born in Genoa is a historical surmise, but most authorities classify it as "almost certain."

What also seems almost certain is that he left his native city and country at a fairly early age, because the first really definite record finds him in Lisbon at the age of twenty-six. He had earlier made several sea journeys to the eastern Mediterranean and to England, and is now known to have put in some part of his youth in the Azores, Cape Verde, and Madeira island groups as a suger buyer representing a large Genoese commercial house.

It was at this occupation that he met and was influenced by many of the outstanding Portuguese navigators of his day. Columbus, contrary to much current public acceptance, was by no means original in his concept that the world could be circumnavigated and that by sailing westward one should be able to reach the riches of the East Indies.

But he has become associated with this radical idea largely because of his tenacity in fighting for the opportunity to prove it. Failing to enlist the support of King John II of Portugal, Columbus moved on once again to another country, Spain, where he spent eight long,

An 18th century map of Spain and the Mediterranean.

agonizing, frustrating years in his attempts to obtain royal backing for his momentous project.

When Columbus finally gained the sponsorship of Queen Isabella and Ferdinand, the coffers of Castile had been emptied by an exhausting war. Fortunately for Columbus, the tiny, obscure fishing village of Palos had been ordered to place two caravels at the Queen's disposal for a year as punishment for engaging in more smuggling than the law would wink at.

Even royal indignation might not have been enough to grant Palos undying fame, if it hadn't been for the Pinzon brothers. Palos was a poor village. But Columbus' patron, Father Juan Perez, appealed to the locally influential Pinzon family to help Christopher. The Pinzons prodded the citizenry into producing the ships and into the equally difficult job of recruiting a crew. Nobody was crazy enough willingly to sign for a voyage *westward* to India.

On Friday, the third of August, 1492, when the crowd on the banks of the River Odiel below Palos waved goodbye to the adventurers, few expected them to return.

Had they been right, the world would have not heard much of the little port of Palos. But today, every school child learns of its existence, and its place in history is assured—all because a Genoese-

Portuguese-Spanish navigator discovered something far greater than he knew and because the townspeople of the tiny community had failed to pay their taxes!

The history of exploration is full of strange turns. One of the queerest is the circumstance that the two greatest voyages made in the name of Spain were commanded by Portuguese seamen who had been turned away by their own countrymen at a time when Portugal was more interested in conquest by sea than ever before in her history; and when Portugal's captains knew more about sea routes, currents and winds than the navigators of any other nation at the time.

When Columbus discovered what he thought to be the Indies by sailing to the West, Ferdinand Magellan was about twelve years old. He grew up amidst the gathering suspicion in Portugal and nearby Spain that Columbus had not discovered the Indies. The few docile red men and meager samples of gold brought back by Columbus represented small proof of the legendary riches of India.

Twelve years later, in October 1504, Magellan signed on as a common seaman for a voyage to India. He stayed in the Orient for more than six years. By the time he returned to Portugal, Columbus had died. But there were still some who believed a route to the Indies could be found westward. Magellan was among them.

He obtained an interview with King Manuel of Portugal. With great enthusiasm, he outlined his plan to the King, but His Majesty wasn't interested.

Magellan joined an expedition in August of 1513 against the Moors to punish them for violation of a treaty. Because he had been wounded during the battle, he was put in charge of the spoils of war, including some cattle. Somebody reported that he tried to turn a little cash for himself by selling the cattle back to the Moors. But Magellan came up with documents clearing him of the charges.

Then came news that Balboa had crossed the Isthmus of Panama and reported an ocean on the other side. Magellan was now more certain than ever that he could find a way to India by sea. Again he approached King Manuel. Again the King gave little attention to the proposal for a new sea route to the wealth of Asia. He remembered only that this man Magellan had been mixed up in a deal with the Moors.

So, at the age of thirty-seven, in 1517, Magellan renounced his Portuguese citizenship and went to Spain.

The times were not friendly to a man with a weird idea about seeking India by the back door. Queen Isabella had died. Her daughter Joanna had returned to Spain after spending many years in Flanders. Her son, the young King Charles, was only a boy with little knowledge or liking for Spain.

Since it was impossible to undertake any expedition to India by *any* route without royal patronage, Magellan tried to enlist the support of Juan de Aranda of the India House, a commercial organization in foreign trade. Aranda finally agreed to arrange an audience with the young King.

The involved intrigue that surrounded Magellan's efforts to obtain the support of young King Charles grew out of the charge by his detractors that he was a "foreigner" and a spy for Portugal! But, like Columbus, Magellan found his most valuable support in a churchman. Just when the project seemed sure to fail, the Bishop of Burgos, who admired and trusted Magellan, went before the King and convinced him that the enterprise was important to the future of Spain.

The King then sent a message to India House in Seville ordering the immediate purchase of a fleet of ships for Magellan. Sr. Aranda went down river to Cadiz and came back with the five vessels authorized by the King's mandate.

It was many months before the little fleet was ready and provisioned for the voyage. The crew was to be 235 men. Provisions included 21,383 pounds of ship's biscuit, plus the usual wine, beans, lentils, dried fish, rice, vinegar and cheese. Also included were 200 barrels of anchovies!

Summer of 1519 and the ships were almost ready to depart. Through the streets of Seville criers went beating their drums, recruiting crews to man the fleet that would sail to the Spice Islands.

Only seventeen men signed up. The sailors of Seville seemed not impressed with the fine theories of Magellan about a new route to the East. There was better pay to be had sailing the known routes to Africa. And far more assurance that they would live to spend their pay.

In Cadiz, the town crier made his proclamation, and in Malaga. Gradually the men signed on. There were Germans, French, English, Basques, Italians from Naples and Genoa, men from the islands of

Corfu, Sicily, Madeira, plus a few Negroes and even some adventurers from Malay.

It was mid-September before everything was ready for sailing. The men were given four months' pay in advance. The cows were brought aboard. Magellan made the final arrangements for his family.

His rights in all the lands he discovered were to go to his son Rodrigo. His wife Doña Beatrice was to receive a pension from India House. The final paragraph of the explorer's will read as follows:

Upon the said day of my burial, three poor men may be clothed, and to each of the three be given a cloak of grey stuff, a cap, a shirt, and a pair of shoes, that they may pray to God for my soul. . . .
    [signed] *Ferdinand Magellan, Commander, His Majesty's Captain-General of the Armada bound for the Spice Islands. . . .*

Magellan's navigation of the bedevilled straits that now bear the great mariner's name is not so well known as the lesser voyages of Columbus. At no spot on the waters of the world is the weather more unfriendly than in those rock-bordered straits at the southern tip of South America. There is no such thing as a "good season" in the straits. Hardly a day passes without rain, snow, hail or heavy winds. The little square-riggers that Magellan took through the straits showed up at their worst in such heavy going. He had no charts, no course to follow but his own iron determination and crude calculations.

Magellan never lived to see Seville again. But before he died on the beach of Macatan Island, whence he had gone to defend the cause of a native King converted by him to the Christian faith, he had taken his little fleet to the shores of the great continent they had sought, India.

Only one ship of that fleet of five returned home. The "Spice Islands" had been found. The men had bartered every possession they had, including their shoes, to fill the vessel with her precious cargo of spices. On Monday, September 8, 1522, the *Victoria* slid into the old quay in the home harbor of Seville. A broadside boomed from every piece of artillery aboard. And the eighteen men who were left of the crews that once numbered 235, went ashore to receive their welcome.

The *Victoria's* cargo sold for such a fabulous price that it more than paid for the cost of the entire three-year expedition. It was a fitting token of the riches the empire of Spain would bring to her shores; a tribute to the man who had said to his commanders as they prepared to board ship three years earlier:

"Follow the flagship, and ask no questions."

The voyages of Columbus and Magellan were a little slow to pay off. But in time they made up for their tardiness. By the middle of the sixteenth century, Spain had become the most powerful nation on earth. She "held dominion over palm and pine" before the English had settled more than a few sparse colonies. Spanish claims included most of the Americas, a large portion of Africa and possessions in Asia. Her kings ruled about half of Europe by one title or another.

But the thundering progress of the conquistadores was equalled only by the earth-shaking collapse of the Spanish Empire.

Under Ferdinand and Isabella, Spanish industry began to develop to meet the demands of colonial trade. The textile industries of Toledo increased employment from 10,000 people to 50,000 people in about twenty-five years. Cloth from Toledo found ready markets: merchants were taking orders five years in advance. Spain began to buy raw silk and manufacture the finished product. Shipbuilding became a leading industry.

But, somehow, the Spanish, like their neighbors the Portuguese, seemed not to have the knack for colonial government. Heavy taxes crippled industry and commerce in the colonies and at home. Even the Spanish farmers were bled into poverty with excessive taxes. For many years, the Moors and the Jews were leaders in Spanish commerce and industry; and when these people were driven from the country, nothing was done to replace their skills and knowledge.

Historians say the ultimate failure of the Spanish empire lay in Spain's inability to establish sound colonial trade. While the English stimulated emigration to the new lands and gave royal grants of land and money, the Spanish discouraged settlement in the new world by their heavy tax demands. They also forbade those who ventured forth to develop local resources or engage in any trade that would compete with the crown. Shipping was restricted to a few specified fleets and strictly specified ports.

By the nineteenth century, the glory of Spain lingered only in the heritage of language spoken in the lands she once held around the world.

PORTUGAL:
Explorers' Haven

THE freshening wind of evening fills the square sails of the little caravel as it pushes westward through the Atlantic. The swarthy pilot standing in the prow smiles at the salt spray flung against his lean face. He looks up at the blue sky. The stars are beginning to shine through. He turns toward the bow of the ship and climbs down the ladder of the fore-deck.

As he crosses the main deck, the seamen rise to return his friendly

The Port of Lisbon, Portugal, c. 1794.

greeting. He clambers up the steps of the half-deck aft and crosses to a small stand. In the center of the stand is the compass. The pilot looks skyward again. His practiced eyes quickly find the bright gleam of the sacred *Stella Maris*, the Pole Star. From a pocket of his jacket he takes a plumb line. Standing behind the compass, he aims his hand at the star and lets the plumb line drop to the compass-card. He notes the point where it strikes. Several times, he repeats the operation, noting the variation between the points where the plumb-bob strikes the compass-card.

From the main deck below, the seamen watch him. He stands with upraised hand, dropping the plumb-bob onto the compass-card again and again to check the bearing of the ship. With this simple ritual, observed each evening by the pilot, men began to free themselves from shore-bound sailing, and struck out into unknown seas. Mariners of the thirteenth century called it "the pilot's blessing." Although centuries earlier, Phoenician navigators had dared with equal courage to sail unknown seas, their secrets of navigation had died with them.

The name of this pilot? Prince Henry of Portugal—known to the world as Henry the Navigator.

If ever a man was wed to the sea, it was this prince of the rugged little maritime nation on the southwest corner of the continent of Europe. When Henry was twenty-two years of age, his father, King John, decided it was time for his sons to win their spurs in the field of battle; so the King financed a crusade against the Moors of Ceuta, across the Straits of Gibraltar on the northern tip of Africa. Henry distinguished himself in this conquest, returning to Lisbon a hero.

But the young prince was one of those people haunted by an idea. During his brief military career in North Africa, he had heard tales of adventure from his Moorish prisoners. They told of great caravans crossing the desert with precious cargoes, of ships that sailed the seas of the Orient, of strange lands beyond the Mediterranean, where fabulous wealth awaited the stout of heart.

Soon after his triumphant return to Lisbon, Henry gathered a few friends and servants and set out for the westernmost point of Europe, the Cape of St. Vincent, at the tip of Portugal. Here, with the Atlantic pounding at him on three sides, he began one of the most important and productive studies of navigation in the history of mankind.

Prince Henry came by his yearning for the deep naturally, many of his ancestors having made their living from the sea. King John, convinced that the destiny of Portugal depended upon her use of the sea, built the fleet of his tiny nation into one of the greatest of the times. He made firm friends with his neighbor nations, with England, Flanders, and the wild Norseland. The enterprise of the English attracted him very much.

He was also attracted by the fair maids of the British Isles, and made one of them his wife. She was Phillipa, daughter of John of Gaunt, the power behind the throne of King Richard II. Little is known of Phillipa but she seems to have been a woman of beauty and wisdom, with a rare capacity for inspiring and guiding her children. No doubt she had much to do with the education of her son, Henry.

Henry had four brothers. The eldest, and heir to the throne, had been given the English name Edward, in honor of his mother's family. He was a likely candidate for the throne, with the highest ideals of knighthood then in fashion. The second son, Pedro, was probably the most brilliant of the family. Like his brother, Henry, he respected scholarship, having both imagination and a love of action. It was Pedro who pushed and prodded other people into taking on the explorations dreamed up by Henry. The other two brothers were John and Fernando. John didn't seem to leave much of a mark on the pages of history. But Fernando, who was deeply religious, became one of the big names in the Catholic history of Portugal when he was martyred by the infidels in Morocco.

When Portuguese Henry began his study of navigation, he went about it in a very practical way. He employed expert navigators, map makers, instrument makers, mathematicians and others to help him gather every scrap of knowledge they could uncover.

Navigation by maps and charts was then beginning to be both a science and an industry. Skilled cartographers were men of importance, and sometimes of wealth. They knew the secret routes that led to adventure and fortune.

But the Prince of Navigators was not satisfied with the little world his map-makers drew. He felt certain that their work was incomplete. He thought perhaps the instruments of navigation might be put to better use to fill out spaces on those fragmentary maps.

As his knowledge of navigation grew, the Prince began to develop the second step in his brilliant career. He established a school at Cape St. Vincent for the education of mariners.

Perhaps the word "school" isn't entirely accurate. Henry simply wanted to improve the maps and instruments of navigation, put the knowledge in the hands of able seamen, and send them off to bring back more knowledge.

The first real discovery made by Henry's "school boys" was the island of Madeira. It was located by Zarco and Teixeira. The Princes divided the island between them and saw that they settled on it with colonists, livestock, seed and other necessities. Before long, Madeira's rich soil was paying big dividends in sugar and wine.

Year after year, Henry pushed his captains down the coast of Africa and outward into the Atlantic, encouraging them to seek and settle new lands.

Late in the year 1460, Henry fell ill and died. Although he was not reputed to be as brilliant as Pedro or Edward, it is his work that launched the age of discovery and exploration which later led to the age of Empire. Because he was a man so firm of character and perseverence, the civilized world is much in his debt.

One of the first navigators to capitalize on the work of Prince Henry was Bartholomew Diaz. Twenty-eight years after the death of Henry, in 1488, the King of Portugal placed Diaz in command of a little fleet of three ships. His orders: to solve the riddle of Africa.

The King had placed on board the ships several African men and women who had been captured in slave raids several years before. They had been converted to Christianity and given rudimentary education. The King instructed Diaz to put them ashore to search for earlier signs of Christian colonies and to develop new holdings for Portugal.

There were two very practical reasons for including women in the shore parties. The first was the obvious one—their singular capacity for increasing the population. The second, according to historians, was that the King thought the natives would not be so quick to massacre a landing party if it included women.

Diaz followed his instructions carefully, as he sailed down the eastern coast of Africa. But after a few stops, a storm struck the little fleet and pushed it out to sea. For thirteen days, the crews battled against the wind and waves. The storm subsided, and they turned their ships toward the East, looking for land. After several more days, Diaz realized that they must have passed beyond the bottom of the dark continent. He promptly ordered the ships to turn back. They found land, then sailed a distance up the east coast of the continent to confirm their hopes. They had discovered the route around Africa to the Indian Ocean!

Diaz was eager to continue on to India, but the discovery that they were in strange and unknown waters was too much for the crew.

They refused to go on. Reluctantly, Diaz agreed to return around the Cape of Good Hope to the port of Lisbon.

Explorers who followed Diaz have been given far better press than he received. Yet he was the one who opened the door to world discovery and colonization. It was his voyage that convinced Portugal's King John II that the route to India's riches and conquest lay around the Cape of Good Hope waiting to be opened by the Portuguese. From Diaz, the little nations on the coast of Europe caught the inspiration for exploration that sent them to the far places of the earth. The charts and instruments and knowledge handed down by Henry the Navigator had at last freed man from the mooring lines of fear that had so long made him cruise timidly close to land.

In addition to discovering the sea route to India, Bartholomeu Diaz found that the tub-like caravels he sailed performed poorly in the heavy seas around the Cape of Good Hope. His reward for this piece of valuable information was an order from the King to supervise the building of a fleet of ships for the planned voyage to India.

These first ships to venture the length and breadth of two of the world's great oceans could hardly be called beautiful, at least not by today's streamlined standards. The little *naus*, as they were called by the Portuguese, were flat-bottomed, with high square stern and bows. Large wales were fastened along the waterline to cut down the rolling of the ships. For armor, each had large planks "two fingers thick" fastened to the sides of the hull. Each also carried naval artillery, twenty guns made of wrought-iron staves bound together with iron hoops. The crew carried crossbows, swords, javelins, axes and boarding pikes.

The holds were divided into three compartments: food was stored forward. Ship's gear amidships, along with potatoes and water. The arsenal occupied the afterhold, with its supply of cannon balls made of stone.

Very likely Diaz could have been the first to land on the fabled shores of India, if his crews hadn't thwarted him. But Vasco da Gama must have full credit for this achievement.

Da Gama's "fleet" consisted of four ships: the *Sao Gabriel, Sao Rafael,* the *Berrio* and a nameless supply ship. They were built in the shipyards on the River Tagus in the port of Lisbon.

It was the summer of the year 1497 when they were completed.

King John II had died two years earlier, to be succeeded by King Manuel. The new King watched the completion of the ships with close attention. He remembered too well the fact that King John II had refused to listen to the ideas of a mariner called Columbus, who had moved on to make some discoveries for Spain in the western waters of the Atlantic. Nothing much had come of them, but King Manuel was going to make certain that Portugal—not Spain or any other nation—captured the riches of far-off India.

On the south bank of the Tagus there stands the little chapel of St. Mary of Bethlehem, built by Prince Henry the Navigator. Since Vasco da Gama's venture was made possible by the achievements of Prince Henry in navigation, he and his crew commended themselves to God's care in solemn Mass at the chapel built by their benefactor.

Oporto, one of the famous ports of the little seafaring island of Portugal.

On the afternoon of July 8, 1497, a wind arose on the Tagus and blew down toward the sea. As the fresh sails were hauled up to catch it, the great red cross painted on each was revealed—the cross of the Order of Christ. The four small ships began to move toward the open sea and toward one of the greatest adventures of that questing era. With them rode a great new destiny for Portugal.

Supplies, as always aboard a ship, were almost as important as the ships themselves. These Portuguese had to plan for a voyage of three years, with little knowledge of how they might be able to replenish. Da Gama's men had a daily ration of one and one-half pounds of hardtack (which bore little resemblance to the delicious waterbiscuit of today), about a pound of salt beef, a little olive oil and vinegar, one and one-fourth pints of wine and two and one-half pints of water.

51

There were lentils, beans, flour, onions and garlic. They also had sugar and honey, and whatever fish they caught themselves.

Da Gama's fleet rounded Good Hope on November twenty-second. He began the voyage up the East coast of Africa, not too sure what he was looking for—or what he was going to find. At the mouth of the Quelimane River, the Portuguese saw the first signs of civilized life. Soon they came to the port of Mozambique, where they saw Arab ships loading in the harbor.

The Moslem ruler of the port received da Gama with royal hospitality, until he found out that his guest was a Christian. The Portuguese had to leave in a hurry.

At Mombassa, the Moslems were all set to entice da Gama into their harbor and destroy his fleet, but the Portuguese were wary. They captured two natives and questioned them. The natives denied any knowledge of a plot against da Gama's fleet, but a few generous ladles of boiling oil applied to their bare hide brought forth the necessary information.

After engaging an Indian pilot at Malindi, above Mombassa, da Gama's fleet set sail for India. On May twentieth, 1498, they dropped anchor at Calicut on the Malabar coast.

The first European ships had reached India.

Calicut was a rich and busy port. The Portuguese were welcomed by the people of India, but not without suspicion. Fuel was added to the fires of distrust by the Arabs who had a corner of the Indian trade, especially the fabulous spice market, and wanted no one to cut in on them.

Da Gama's gifts of striped cloths, hats, hoods, strings of coral, sugar, oil and honey which he brought to the local ruler met with scornful refusal. The Arabs took every advantage they could of his lack of knowledge of the country and the people. Moslem merchants refused to buy the Portuguese cargoes. Da Gama finally managed to dispose of most of his goods, but only at meager prices. Late in August, he set sail for home, with little more than samples of the spices and other riches which would one day finance the founding of the first world empire—the empire of Portugal.

Thus, although Diaz supplied the first knowledge that there was a route to India around the lower end of Africa, to da Gama must go the credit for changing the course of the history of Europe and Asia. He confirmed the classic tradition of the great wealth of India. He consigned the whole of the Mediterranean, the ancient center of sea trade, to second place. For nearly four centuries, until the opening of the Suez Canal, all ships eastbound followed the route of da Gama from Europe.

Beside the achievements of Diaz and da Gama, the discovery made by Columbus several years earlier seemed insignificant. Columbus had brought back no spices, no jewels: he found a few naked savages. Da Gama's cargoes may have been sparse, but he saw palaces ornate with gold and ivory and precious stones. Columbus saw nothing but grass huts. The fleets that followed da Gama's course to India returned laden with wealth, and da Gama himself did better the next time around, but it was generations before the discovery of Columbus produced pay dirt.

The voyage to India was perhaps the greatest feat of navigation man had ever achieved up to that day. Columbus had favoring winds most of the time; his voyage was made directly across a single ocean. Da Gama's rough voyage lasted twenty-six months. The voyage of Columbus took only a few weeks.

For a few years, Portugal seemed content to develop her trade with the East, letting conquest lie idle. As gradually military conquest was used to protect sea commerce, Portuguese port colonies grew in Africa, Asia and South America. But it takes a navy, armies and experienced colonial administrators to manage a world empire. Portugal was still poor, relatively a tiny nation. She was no fair match for the complex responsibilities brought home by her bold seamen.

Portugal was doomed from the start to fail her great opportunity. She was a "pilot run" for empires to come. The long voyages to India were costly, both in money and men and Portugal had little of either. Her ruling class had no experience in colonial government. Her bankers had neither sufficient funds nor the experience to manage international trade on a grand scale beyond anything ever attempted before.

Soon the experienced financial experts of Germany, the Low Countries, and Italy began to buy into the India expeditions of Portugal. Because of their superior finances, they could command first mortgages on returning cargoes. The wealth of India began to trickle out of Lisbon into other ports. It was not long until Antwerp replaced the Portuguese port as the center of the spice trade in Western Europe.

PART 4

Ports and People
of Great Britain

LONDON:
Base of Empire

TIME gathers its legions of years and days at the Port of London. History was made here—not just English history, but world history. More globe-affecting events have had their origin in ancient, medieval and modern times right on the banks of the Thames than in any other port of the world.

They were events that led to the growth of international commerce, to discoveries, to colonization, to the building of finer and bigger ships, to battle, to victory or defeat, to happy results or to tragic eventualities. Western European trade-routes—world trade itself indeed—began here in the days when the soil of Britain still resounded to the departing footsteps of her once Roman conquerors, leaving the poor Britons to the mercies of other invaders, to lament their departure, and to plead for the Romans' return.

56

A view of London Dock, c. 1808.

When the legions of Julius Caesar cautiously pushed their trim galleys up the Thames more than two thousand years ago, they found a small Celtic settlement called Llyn-Din—a trading center.

The location appealed to the colony-minded Romans: it was protected by being more than fifty miles from the sea, a distance that made the town close enough for the purpose of commerce to the great navigable rivers of the Continent—the Scheldt, the Rhine, the Seine, the Elbe.

There is a tradition that this London-in-embryo had come into being as a by-product of the salt trade between the Tight Little Island and the Continent. An ancient trade route passed along where Westminster Abbey now stands near the river banks. When the spring and fall rains came to swell the old river out of her shores, the pack trains bearing salt had to wait until low water made it possible to cross. A little settlement thus sprang up on the river shore to care for the freight and the traders. A community warehouse was put up—the first of its kind. And thus, so it is claimed by some, London began. Whether true or not, the Romans called the town they found there Londinium.

Expert colonizers though they were, the Romans didn't do too well with England. But before finally bidding goodbye to the shores of England sometime in the fifth century, they prepared defenses at the mouth of the Thames against those Teutonic pirates, the Anglo-Saxons. But all the defenses in the world could not hold back the race of men whose ships, centuries later, sailing out of this same Thames River, were to make England mistress of the seas.

The seafaring Anglo-Saxons started at once to build up trade with the continent whence they had come. From the London settlement, the long-oared Saxon ships went down the Thames and over to the mainland of Europe. Next, the sea-minded Danes, enviously eyeing Britain, decided to capture the port of London. But good King Alfred the Great outsmarted them, drove them out and the little port remained Anglo-Saxon.

Then Alfred, earliest English King to realize the importance of foreign commerce to England, set about developing London as a sea-port city. He encouraged the construction of docks and ships and promoted the study of navigation. Under his reign, London first grasped her potentialities as a major center of sea power.

Wool from the flocks of English sheep grazing on English hillsides and in English meadows has always played a vital part in the history of Port London. Edward III, coming to the throne in the fourteenth century, used wool in his own version of a "cold war." At first, he encouraged free trade, inviting merchants of other nations to market their goods in England. But in order to put a crimp in the trade of his enemies on the continent, Edward changed his policies and in time clamped down hard on the import of clothing into England.

Since the clothmakers of Flanders depended almost entirely on English wool, their industry fell apart overnight. Edward, betting that this would happen, now began to offer safe conduct and employment to Flemish weavers. The weavers took him up, promptly moved to England and there began the great woolen trades that are now famous the world over.

The third Edward didn't stop there. He set sail down the Thames with a fleet of merchant ships decked out as vessels of war. At Sluys he met the object of his conquest—a French fleet—and lambasted it soundly.

Edward's sea victory over France brought about a boom in ship-building along the Thames. London enacted a law requiring all cargoes—both imports and exports—to be carried in English ships. From the end of the thirteenth century, when London got a royal charter of incorporation, the city began to act as a kind of port authority for the entire realm. Late in the sixteenth century, Edward IV granted Port London a number of important commercial rights, perhaps the most important of which was the right to weigh, measure and warehouse all wools brought down to the port. The right also was granted to check the cargoes of all departing ships and determine what was what. London port men could measure wine—a pleasant duty, one might imagine—clean spices and pack goods properly for shipment.

Other statutes followed, compelling Italian merchants to sell all their goods in England at wholesale prices and to use the money they made to buy English products. No foreigners could deal in wool. Merchants from other countries had to stay in specified lodgings. Shrewd legislation it was, too, leading to continued growth of the Port's business.

Edward VII—first of the sturdy Tudors—is sometimes called the first business-minded King of England. Very actively he pushed ship-building and provided for the protection of British shipping interests by issuing strong decrees against traders from other countries. His efforts were not entirely successful because the foreign traders finally rebelled and prices went up on products England needed. But he made a good beginning and his successors built upon his foundation.

Historians pay so much attention to the too-colorful private life of Henry VIII that we hear little of the real advances in trade and sea power made in his reign. It was the bluff and burly Henry who sponsored the Royal Naval Dockyards at Woolwich and Deptford, and set out to develop a naval fleet for England. It was a most important step in the growth of British sea supremacy and a threat to Spain, pre-eminent then as the greatest power on land and sea.

By 1500, the voyages of Columbus and other navigators of his time

had turned the thoughts of Englishmen toward the uncharted lands beyond the sea horizons of their native waters. The discovery of a route to India around the Cape of Good Hope added fuel to the fire of their imaginations. Fleets for exploration and colonization began to set out from London.

On a late spring day in 1553, two great London-built ships hoisted sail and made their way down the Thames, followed by a smaller vessel. First sailed *Bona Speranza*, followed by *Edward Bonaventure*. Last followed *Bona Confidentia*.

On the deck of *Bona Speranza*, the flagship, stood Sir Hugh

The famous London Pool, 1843.

Willoughby, of Nottingham, recently chosen by the London Company of Merchant Adventurers to find that much-sought-for northwest passage to China. Second in command was the famous Richard Chancellor, a wealthy seaman who had led many successful commercial voyages for England.

Gallant but ill-starred, this expedition never found a northwest passage, but after nearly a year at sea, the flagship *Bona Speranza* reached the Lapland coast. There Willoughby and his crew perished. Chancellor, however, went on to enter the White Sea and make his way down to Moscow.

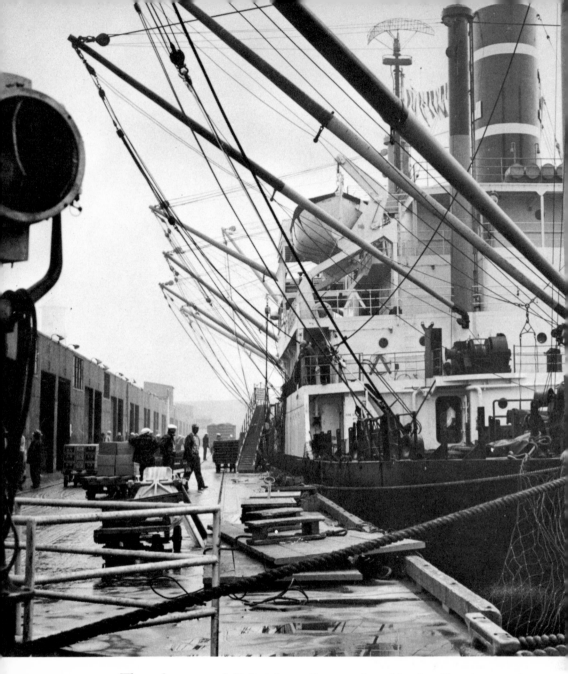

There he opened Britain's earliest trade with the Russians and
established the basis for the successful ventures of the London Muscovy Company, incorporated by Queen Mary in 1555. The next year,
however, Chancellor, making the return trip from Moscow bringing
to England a passenger of great importance—the first Russian Ambassador to the Court England—ran afoul of bad weather. A blinding
storm struck the *Edward Bonaventure* and wrecked her near Aberdeen,
with the loss of captain, crew and passengers.

Busy wharves in London today.

London's Muscovy Company survived and fostered many other such famous commercial firms of adventure. There was the Turkey Company, the African Company and later the New England and Virginia Companies. But the greatest of all the British trading companies, of course, was the East India Company.

When the voyages of Vasco da Gama established for Portugal an Empire in the East, the British in London Port began to look toward the rising sun. But the Dutch also sent Cornelius Houtman around

63

the Cape with four ships in 1595 to lay the foundations of a Dutch Empire of the East. Hearing of it, the English knew they would be in for trouble should the Dutch try to carve out an Eastern empire for themselves.

The British East India Company thereupon received a right royal charter, including a fifteen-year monopoly on trade with India and exemption from port duty for the first four voyages. The natural caution of capital investors, however, prompted them to go slowly. They recalled the tales of great storms around the Cape; the ability of the Dutch and the Portuguese to defend their rights against all comers. The new East India Company meanwhile was trying to raise funds for an expedition of six ships. Finally they had to settle for five: an ancient provision craft named the *Guest*; a privateer, *Red Dragon*—built by the Earl of Cumberland at London to capture Spanish cargoes—and the *Hector, Ascension* and *Susan*.

The expedition made its way down the Thames under the command of James Lancaster, worthy London shipmaster, on the quarterdeck. After a rough voyage around the Cape and across the Indian Ocean the little fleet dropped anchor at the Dutch-occupied port of Acheen in Sumatra. Sick and enervated, Captain Lancaster and his men nevertheless prepared to defend themselves and their ships from the Dutch. To their amazement, they were received with generous Dutch hospitality—another instance of mutual commercial aspiration, leading in time to international friendship.

Rested from their sea ordeal, the British adventurers put to sea again, but not before expressing their appreciation to the Dutch: as evidence of their sincerity, the Britons promptly captured a rich Portuguese ship *Soa Thome,* instead of a temptingly fat and heavily laden Dutch merchantman, lying close at hand, bound for Rotterdam.

Lancaster's expedition went on to Java. There he set up a trading station for future voyages. Investors in the enterprise doubled both their money and their enthusiasm for the riches of the East. The East India trade was on!

But it was some years earlier that the stage for this successful operation had been set, with the colorful and magnetic personality of the great Elizabth I serving as stage manager!

For British sea power would never have been able to provide the safety of the high seas to British commercial fleets had it not been for

A great ocean liner from New Zealand docks at London.

A view of the Tilbury Docks on the Thames.

the dramatic events of August 5, 1588, a memorable date in the history of England and of the world.

The British had known for some time that Spain expected to make an invasion of their island and an attack upon their chief city. When the huge but cumbersome Spanish ships actually hove up the Channel, the fast heavily-armed home-built little vessels of John Hawkins of London Port went out to meet the invaders. Drake, Raleigh, Frobisher and Howard pitted their skill against the sea forces of the powerful King of Spain.

Ready, that morning four centuries ago, to board the English ships,

17,000 volunteers had gathered at Tilbury to defend their Queen and their shores. England had no standing army to use for such a purpose. Elizabeth, shrewd and tight-fisted, would not spend the money for such a purpose; she felt that at the first notes of the bugle "an army of young patriots would flock to the colors." In this instance Elizabeth was proved right. The volunteers came with a rush—dandies from the streets, gentlemen from the court, tradesmen from their offices and shops, weavers from their looms, tanners from their stinking yards, landlubbers of all descriptions. These were the defenders of Queen and homeland. The Earl of Leicester had rallied them and they were

67

ready to go and smash the Spaniards. Earlier, Leicester—the Queen's then favorite—had urged her to visit the troops: "You shall comfort not only these thousands but many more who shall hear of it." So down came Elizabeth to Tilbury by barge. As she set foot upon the quay, cannon roared in royal salute. Fifes shrilled. Drums rolled. A thousand horse and two thousand foot soldiers escorted the wilful red-headed monarch as she spoke "man to man" to her country's defenders.

Imperious, brooking no interference with what she conceived to be her royal right, rather sharp in her dealings, but brave beyond most women of history and able to inspire by her words and presence a loyalty such as Englishmen had not hitherto known, Elizabeth has sent her words ringing down through the centuries:

My loving people, we have been persuaded by some that are careful of our safety, to take heed how we commit ourselves (Our Royal person) to armed multitudes for fear of treachery; but I assure you I do not live in distrust of my faithful and loving people.

Let tyrants fear! . . . I have placed my chiefest strength and safeguard in the loyal hearts and goodwill of my subjects. I am come among you . . . being resolved in the midst and heat of battle to live and die amongst you all; to lay down for my God, and for my Kingdom, and for my people, my honour and my blood even in the dust . . .

The day following Elizabeth's arrival Leicester's troops drew up in serried lines across the parade ground for inspection by their Queen. One historian reports that she walked up and down the line "sometimes with a martial pace, sometimes like a woman."

Just to what extent Elizabeth did actually mingle with her troops on that day seems to have got lost in legend, a legend created by the ballad-maker who wrote of it, and the artist who painted a picture of the Queen riding her royal charger at Tilbury. This is the ballad:

> *The Sergeant trumpet with his mace,*
> *And nine with trumpets after him,*
> *Bareheaded went before her Grace*
> *In coats of scarlet trim.*
>
> *Then came the Queen on prancing steed,*
> *Attired like an angel bright*

And eight brave footmen at her feet
Whose jerkins were most rich in sight . . .

Her faithful soldiers, great and small.
Each stood by within his place,
Upon their knees began to fall,
Desiring God to "Save Her Grace!"
For joy whereof her eyes were filled
That the water down distilled . . .

The 17,000 volunteers gathered at Tilbury, whose loyalty brought tears to the eyes of their Queen, were never called upon to defend her. The Spanish Armada was shattered and scattered to the winds. Elizabeth's England was mistress of the seas. Her Port of London remained the port of the world.

Those who come to London today on a passenger liner land at this very Tilbury, about twenty-five miles below the big city. The present docks were built by the East and West Indian Dock Company in 1886: four miles of quays, a drydock big enough for the large ships to enter the port, a floating landing stage, twenty-nine acres of transit sheds and rail terminals.

Before that floating landing stage was built, ships anchored in midstream and passengers came ashore via tender. But today, some of the

Wool from New Zealand at the Royal Docks, London.

large liners themselves discharge both passengers and cargo on docks at every stage of the tide.

Tilbury today handles traffic from India; from the Fast East, from Indonesia, the Persian Gulf, West Africa; from the West Indies; from Australia. Cargoes in Tilbury transit sheds include hides, rubber, gum, tea, jute, hemp, carpets and wool.

A few miles above Tilbury, at Woolwich Reach, are the Royal Victoria and Albert, and the George V docks. Even though the sail-

BRITISH INFORMATION SERVICES

Aerial view of the Royal Docks.

ing ships are gone, the river will always bear their signature in its nomenclatures of locale—Gravesend Reach, Gallions Reach, Blackwall Reach, Limehouse Reach. (A "reach" is the distance a sailing ship could travel on the river before it had to shift sails to catch the wind from another angle and send it around a bend.) These tremendous docks claim the largest area of impounded water in the world, 235 acres.

The Royal Victoria Dock was built in 1855, the Royal Albert in

King George V Dock, London.

1880, the King George in 1921. Royal Docks handle meat, dairy produce and tobacco, Australian lamb, and butter from New Zealand.

London port today has a mighty tobacco trade; mostly shipments from America. England's wool industry has been a major item of Port London since the Saxon days. British woolens, tweeds and cheviots are today known and coveted everywhere and are stored on the London docks that can handle more than 200,000 bales. Here occurs the fore-

most "wool show" of all time—in showrooms that face the northern light, giving the merchants an opportunity to inspect the wares under ideal conditions that show texture, weave, warp and woof. Not only is there wool from the British Isles, but from New Zealand, South Africa and South America as well.

There are 350 varieties of wool—and the men of London Port can differentiate among them all.

73

At St. Katherine's docks, there are sales of ivory tusks that come from Africa to London.

London Tower is spang up against St. Katherine's wharf. The Tower is inevitably a unit of the Port of London, if for no other reason than that long ago barges would dock at the foot of its mossy dank stairs and some unfortunate passenger enter at the Traitors' stairs. Most likely he, or she, would come out in a box, headless.

So the thriving Port of London of today is the historic result of

Royal Albert Dock, London.

the adventures, the courage, the determination, the imagination and the intelligence of a motley group of individuals who have lived and worked in the bustling city since the beginnings of recorded history.

They have created a virtual kaleidoscope of brilliant color—regal monarchs and humble weavers, lordly knights and lowly seamen, beautiful women and gallant warriors, shrewd businessmen and stout yeomen. All have combined, in greater or less measure to contribute to the greatness that is the Port of London—base of empire.

BRITISH INFORMATION SERVICES

Other British Ports

*L*IVERPOOL lacks the charm of Naples or Venice. It has none of the turbulent history of the Portuguese or Spanish ports. It does not reflect the tradition that imparts a special aura to London.

Yet Liverpool is the major export center of the British Commonwealth. Last year, goods worth nearly a half billion pounds sterling (about $1,250,000,000) cleared the docks of Liverpool on their way to other seaports throughout the world.

Liverpool is old. The first recognition of the city's importance as a port came in 1207, when King John granted the city its original charter. For several centuries the port continued to be a minor shipping center. Little ships plied between its docks and the adjacent English ports and to Ireland, France and Spain. Fish and wool made up its major exports; wines and irons, its principal imports.

The Liverpool Waterfront, 1841.

The advent of industrial revolution, however, and the development of the Lancashire cotton industry brought increased trade with America and the West Indies.

Liverpool's real growth and importance as a major world port began with the development of steamship companies. In 1840 Cunard's little ship *Britannia* set out from Liverpool and arrived in Boston—the first Cunarder to make the trip. The first to establish regular liner service, the *Britannia* had wooden paddlewheels, auxiliary sails, a long jib-boom and a cow on board to supply fresh milk for passengers. She displaced 1,100 tons—the ship, not the cow.

The first iron steamers with screw propellers sailed from Liverpool in 1852. But they were pioneers, somewhat ahead of their time and most passengers proved unwilling to risk crossing the ocean on ships propelled by a piece of machinery so far under water they couldn't see it. In deference to this timidity, Cunard built two more iron paddlewheel steamers, *Persia* and *Scotia*, thus assuring their passengers they were pushed along by some visible means of propulsion.

Liverpool's importance as a passenger port of embarkation for America rose high during the early and middle years of the last century. Unrestricted immigration admitted to the United States millions of newcomers bent upon seeking new homes and making new lives for themselves.

Since the preponderance of this immigrant traffic was from nearby Scotland and Ireland, shipping companies using Liverpool profited enormously in their steerage and third class trade carrying this type of passenger. New companies, seeking a share in the immigration money, moved in, set up their shipping headquarters and opened terminals in the big smoky city on the Mersey. Before long the city had bred

PEABODY MUSEUM OF SALEM

and fostered a race of waterfront workers: hard, bluff, skilled in their craft, honest and dependable.

Frequently a shipload of young Irish girls seeking escape from harsh, restrictive laws or unhappy family conditions at home, and embarking to find work as domestics in America, lived at the same string of waterfront boarding houses as those which housed the stevedores. Often these girls were detained in port for several weeks, waiting for their ships. And youth being what it is—whether in old Liverpool or in modern New York City—romantic liaisons frequently resulted.

Many an Irish maid, sailing for Boston or other ports in the new world, married "above her station" in America, settled down and founded a family that made a good name for itself.

Typical of nineteenth century Liverpool is the romantic story of Mike Monohan and his Cathleen. Mike was a stevedore. Soon with his native knack for friendliness, he'd organized a group of other steve-

Another view of old Liverpool.

dores to work for him on contract jobs for loading and unloading ships.

Time was moving prosperously along. Mike continued to make friends with the shipmasters for whom he worked. The waterfront charmed him—the ships from Boston intrigued him particularly, especially one, the great *Beacon Hill*. Her captain, Hezekiah Sprague, for whom Mike did a job or two, told the boy stories of the United States, of Boston, of the opportunities there for bright and ambitious young men.

"Why not come with me and try your luck in America?" inquired Captain Sprague.

Mike shook his head. He was doing all right here in Liverpool. "I'm thankin' ye, Captin, but me job here's safe and stiddy. I'm makin' me way along. It's loath I'd be to give it up."

One day when the *Beacon Hill* rested, light, in a wet dock, a heavy squall came roaring up the Mersey, slapping her broadside, heeling her over to port, her mighty spars crashing into a nearby warehouse. Ruefully the Captain examined his ship.

"It's a bad business, Mike," the captain said.

"Shure, and not so bad, Captin," Mike returned cheerfully. "I'll get me bhyes here in a minute and we'll have her soon on an even keel agin."

So with lines and tackle and capstan and other nautical gear, Mike's gang, aided by the *Beacon Hill's* crew, soon had the ship to rights once again.

"Mike," said Captain Sprague, shaking his hand, "I'm deeply grateful to you."

"Faith and 'tis nothing," Mike responded. "Anytime at all!"

"Why don't you make that trip with me to Boston as my guest?"

Again Mike grinned and shook his head. But this time the shake was not so vigorous as formerly. "Well now Captin—thankin' you kindly—I may be doing that very thing before long."

"Let me know, then. I'll be back in a month or two." And the two friends parted with mutual esteem.

Now, what Mike did not tell the Captain was that something had happened to turn his thoughts seriously toward America. Romance had entered Mike's life. Only a few days before he'd gone to his boarding house for dinner and found a group of young Irish girls at table, waiting to sail to America. Many of them were doubtless pretty, but Mike had eyes only for one—Cathleen O'Hearn—not long out of County Clare. Mike made her acquaintance, and before long they had become close friends. As he thought, he found that she would give the back of her hand to a stevedore or to anyone else who tried to make what might be called, in those days, improper advances.

"Stay here in Liverpool with me, darlin! Marry me and we'll be making our home here," he pleaded. But Cathleen had ideas of her own.

"It's to the new world I'm started, and I'll stop not one mile short of it!" she announced with a stubbornness that matched his own. Mike continued to press his suit; Cathleen continued to refuse. Yes, she finally admitted, she did love him and hoped someday they would meet and marry beyond the seas. Beyond that statement she would not go.

The *Beacon Hill* finally departed, Cathleen among its passengers. Both young people, adamant to the last, took a fond farewell of each other—Cathleen waving from a porthole near the stern as Mike sadly turned back to his work.

Months passed. Back came Captain Sprague and the *Beacon Hill*.

"How about it, Mike? Want to make that trip with me this time?" And, his heart full of yearning for the girl who had left him behind, Mike answered:

"I'll take ye up on it this time Captin, thank ye kindly, sor!" He may or may not have told Captain Sprague of the girl in America he hoped to find. Although Boston was then a city of 75,000, Mike probably thought of it as a village where he would be able to ask the first man he met, "Can ye tell me, me buck, where I can find Miss Cathleen O'Hearn?" and get the right answer.

Mike made a good trip to Boston and Captain Sprague took him on as a coachman until he could find a job in his own field of endeavor.

One morning Captain Sprague announced at the breakfast table: "I want you to drive me over to Mr. Daniel Webster's home, Green Harbor, this morning, Mike."

"Will it be meself getting a chance to see him?" Mike asked in a voice of awe and reverence. Mike had been hearing of the great American orator and statesman ever since he had boarded ship for America; of the great Webster's powerful word battles in the Senate with brilliant Calhoun and Clay, and other giants of his time, and how the God-like Daniel nearly always came out the winner.

"You might, at that," the captain told him with a smile. Captain Sprague lived by the North River on the south shore of Boston, famous as the "river of a thousand ships." As they drove along the shore behind a pair of spanking high-stepping bays, Mike's eyes eagerly devoured the activities on the waterfront and decided that life here in America would be pleasant after all—provided he could find his sweetheart.

On they drove, through the big gateway, a stately semicircular driveway. Soon they drew up in front of the Webster house.

"Drive around to the side entrance, Mike, and wait for me."

Then while Mike sat there in the carriage waiting, dreaming of the future, the notes of a song came floating out to him from inside the house. He knew the song—"Peg In A Low-Back Car"—had known it from childhood. And the voice! No one could have that voice but Cathleen O'Hearn. Many a time as they had walked along the Liverpool docks she'd sung it for him in her clear naturally sweet soprano, and he'd rumbled along in a semblance of baritone.

"Cathleen, me darlin'!" Mike yelled out at the top of his voice. He jumped from the carriage, dashed into the house, and there he found her—Cathleen herself, head done up in a cloth, feather duster in her hand, sadness in her eyes—until she recognized Mike!

Out came Captain Sprague and Mr. Webster, astounded at the ruckus, to find the young couple locked in a fond embrace. Explanations followed. So pleased was Senator Webster with the romance that he aided Mike in finding employment on the Boston waterfront.

When the couple married, he provided one of the houses on his estate for them to occupy. It is to be supposed that they lived happily ever after. At any rate this couple, who met between ships at Liverpool, have descendants to the third and fourth generation living in New England today.

Southampton is the aristocrat of European seaports. There dock the prestige ships in the lucrative North Atlantic trade, but that was not always the case. Back in the 1840's and 1850's, when the first steam-propelled ships began regularly to negotiate the North Atlantic, Liverpool was the most convenient terminal to the United

States which was wide open to unrestricted immigration. The port of Liverpool lies nearer Ireland, Scotland and Wales (whence came, then, the bulk of the emigrants to seek new homes and lives over here) than any other English port. With the new century and its laws restricting immigration to our country, the emigrant trade fell off and passenger ships began to land at Southampton, which is nearer London than is Liverpool.

The tidal conditions at Southampton, too, are far more favorable for huge modern ships than are those of Liverpool. Southampton has what is called a tripod harbor. If you cut the first wedge from a pumpkin pie and draw it an inch away from the whole, leaving it still in its relatively normal position, you will have a fairly good illustration of the shape of Southampton's port and harbor. Up the right side of the Isle of Wight (the pie wedge) flows a channel known as Spithead. Up the left hand side, runs a channel known as the Solent. Now imagine another long, narrow body of water running from the apex of the angle from which you cut the wedge, straight into the city of Southampton and you will have an understandable though crude picture of what makes Southampton valuable as the port for the world's largest and most luxurious ships.

To most people, Southampton is a gateway—and merely that—into England. London lies up there only fifty miles ahead, beckoning. But Southampton has its own points of interest. It is ancient. Its history and its historical connotations go far back into antiquity.

The Romans came early to Southampton—led by one of the subordinate commanders of Julius Caesar. The Lion-Hearted Richard, with his forces, set out from Southampton to fight Saladin in one of the Crusades. Edward III started with a fleet from Southampton in an effort to make good his claim to the French throne through his grandfather at the Battle of Crecy. King Henry V and his army went down from Southampton to fight and win at Agincourt a victory and a lovely French bride.

But for us Americans, Southampton holds this special appeal. The *Mayflower*, bearing the Pilgrims-to-be, sailed down the Solent along this same course which modern liners sail today, on an August day in 1620. Finally she disappeared in the mists of the Atlantic, her prow headed towards the New World.

On her afterdeck one can very well imagine the stalwart figure of young John Alden—he of the "Why-don't-you-speak-for-yourself-John" fame—watching with homesick eyes the fast-disappearing shore of Southampton. For the city was John's home. His father's farm lay near the water.

John was a first-rate cooper—a maker of barrels which were known to hold together regardless of their contents. The Pilgrims took him along because of that skill, although one cannot help wondering why the abstemious Pilgrims wanted a cooper.

Southampton got its name from the old Saxon word, Hamtun, which means simply "Home Town." How it so happened that another settlement to the north had already taken that name, so *this* settlement called itself Southamtun, or Southamton. Within the town proper there are some points of interest.

The city is woven in with the name of one of England's earliest strong Kings—Canute, the Dane. During his youthful years Canute proved to be cruel and dictatorial. Later in life he mellowed and

Dover, England, 1822.

COURTESY, THE MARINERS MUSEUM, NEWPORT NEWS, VA.

learned to love England better than the Denmark he had left, and to work for her welfare. In Southampton the house in which Canute lived—or at least the site of it—can still be seen.

Southampton has an interesting street known as Blue Anchor Lane. On this street stood King John's house, abutting on the wall. Farther down the street, along the same wall are Watergate Tower, the remains of Windwhistle Town and Cathchcold Tower.

Shortly after the Norman invasion, William the Conqueror, then safely astride the English throne, decided to take action that would guarantee that channels of trade would be kept open.

He proceeded to make an agreement with five English seaport towns to provide him with fifty-seven ships, free of all costs, which were to remain in his service for a stated period of years. The five towns— Dover, Sandwich, Hastings, Romney and Hythe—became known as the Cinque Ports, a name which they collectively retain to this day.

In return for their ships, the communities received exemption from

BRITISH INFORMATION SERVICES

A ship entering the Glasgow docks.

all taxes, the right to set up their own courts, the right to impose their own taxes and the right to pass certain types of laws! In effect, they were virtually autonomous.

But William lived to regret his largesse. The barons of the Cinque Ports took every possible advantage of their special status, disregarding court edicts, engaging in piracy against other British ports and generally claiming immunity from all royal control.

The Cinque Ports flourished for a while, but their importance diminished rapidly with the beginning of the thirteenth century, as Port London began to assume greater and greater growth.

Glasgow on the Clyde in Scotland is one of the greatest shipbuilding centers in the world. The city has a million plus population and dates her founding back to the sixth century. Though she lacks the historic patina of Edinburgh, she has her art museums, her universities and colleges. The largest of all her industries is the shipbuilding at Glasgow Port, Clydebank and Greenock nearby.

Americans have a particular connection with Glasgow, since many of the larger and finer ships entering New York harbor today were built there. It was Sam Cunard who, back in 1840, established the first regular steamship service between the United States port of

87

Boston and Glasgow. His earliest steamer—the little *Britannia*, with her chunking engines, her flapping side paddles, her auxiliary sail to help the engines along, and a cow on board to supply the passengers with fresh milk—was built in Glasgow. She was only 207 feet long.

Tobacco from America opened the River Clyde to shipping. Steel and steam engines kept it open.

Before the American Colonies revolted against England, sailing ships laden with tobacco from Virginia and the Carolinas crossed the Atlantic to the mouth of the Clyde. There they transferred their cargoes to lighters for transport into the city of Glasgow. By 1772, half the tobacco imported into the United Kingdom was coming in through Glasgow. But lighterage was slow and costly. The wealthy tobacco merchants wanted fast efficient handling of their produce. They promoted the dredging of the shallow Clyde to permit vessels to approach close to the banks of the river. The construction of docks and warehouses followed. Glasgow was on its way to become a major port.

It was about 1801 that the Scottish shipbuilder Symington built a little steamer called the *Charlotte Dundas*. She was put to work at towing barges on the Foss and Clyde Canal. As she whoofed busily up and down the canal, a young American stood on the banks and watched.

His name was Robert Fulton. With what he had seen locked in his mind, he returned home to America to experiment with a steamer of his own on the Hudson River.

Although Glasgow shipwrights turned out some of the best-remembered wooden sailing craft—like the *Cutty Sark*—their fame has been written on the seas with steal and steam.

Destiny seems to have selected Glasgow to seal the doom of the sailing ships. The rich coal fields in the hills beyond the Clyde nourished the growth of the iron and steel industry, just as the forests of tall trees on American shores nourished the sailship industry. Steel from the Glasgow mills went into the rugged ships that soon made wooden ships little more than a romantic memory.

The first sizeable merchant ship of steel—the *Botomahan*—was built by Denny on the Clyde in 1879 for the Union Steamship Line of New Zealand. Less than half a century later—in 1924—the Union Steamship Line made maritime history again, with the launching of the *Aorangi* at the Clyde Fairfield Yard on the Clyde. The *Aorangi* was the first large passenger ship to carry a diesel engine.

But the crowning glory of Glasgow shipbuilders remains the building of the great "Queens" for Cunard.

Riggers at work on a British ship.

PART 5

Some Other Ports, Some Other People

Ports and People of Western Europe

Cardinal richelieu was certain that his beloved France had a great future in sea trade. He said, "France, bounded by two seas, can maintain herself only by sea power."

He encouraged the development of colonial companies and built up the navy, while his British neighbors called him the "fresh water admiral." During the first half of the seventeenth century, when Dutch trade and sea power were flourishing, the French had more than twenty commercial companies around the world—in the Malay states, India, Madagascar, Africa, the West Indies, Guinea and Canada. Investing in colonial enterprises became fashionable—not to mention profitable—among the nobility. The government backed them to the hilt. Young men discharged from the army and navy were sold a bill of goods on the great opportunities in far-away lands.

Young girls from poor families were transported free of charge to the colonies.

For a while the companies and the colonies prospered. But the self-appointed "Great Monarch" of France, Louis XIV, wanted more elbow room at home. He was determined to take over Spain and Portugal on the South, and everything between himself and the North Sea. The income from his colonies was dissipated on wars with his neighbors.

Piece by piece, France lost her holdings on continental North America to the English. Others in the West Indies and Africa slipped away. The idea of colonial expansion became distasteful to the French people. They blamed their troubles at home on the failures of the colonies—and the failures of their colonies on their troubles at home.

LE HAVRE

W ORLD WAR II brought to Normandy and Brittany the greatest invasion in military history, sweeping westward to the sea. The postwar years have witnessed another type of invasion—*from* the sea—which has continued as the ports of Le Havre, Cherbourg, and Brest have become increasingly the gateways for a mounting number of visitors from America and other continents. Now, at almost any season of the year, and especially in the spring and summer, they debark by the tens of thousands from transatlantic liners to visit or revisit this territory famed for centuries in literature, legend and world history.

It reached its historic peak in the world's greatest war. Because this channel-bordering land was where the forces of the free world breached the defenses of Fortress Europe, the seaports of Western France have become tourist meccas of the Western World. Le Havre, virtually rebuilt in its entirety, stands now as the number one passenger seaport of France.

One finds it today a vastly different city from the port which welcomed the world traveler only twenty years ago at the time the Germans marched into Poland. When the long struggle ended in 1945, those who appraised the broken and battered French nation agreed that Le Havre was the hardest hit seaport in all Western Europe. Quays, piers, docks, warehouses, transit sheds, bunkering stations, drydocks, repair yards—Le Havre had had them all and 1945 saw them turned into a shambles of twisted, seemingly useless wreckage—the port a graveyard for ships of every size and type.

In the city itself more than 12,000 buildings fell victim to the attacking Germans. Shells also from Allied ships and, above all, from the almost continuous high- and low-level bombing to which British and American air power subjected the city, played unspeakable additional havoc. Look at the war-time pictures of the city which you may see in the museums of Le Havre today. You will gain a realizing sense of the agony endured. Indeed, it may seem to you that the great flanking white cliffs which stand like gateposts to the broad estuary of the Seine were the only things that managed to survive intact those fierce bombings and invasions.

These cliffs, studded with the remains of German fortification and monuments to those who reduced those barriers at so vast a sacrifice, rise even higher into the sky than their more famous counter-parts at Dover and along the English coast beyond the Channel.

But Le Havre could not stay dead.

In present-day Le Havre, you find a city rebuilt, noisy with com-merce. Many of the ancient houses and buildings which had been treasured from the thirteenth century are gone. Despite the losses of ancient landmarks, however, you will be shown with pride the modern new twenty-story city hall—a skyscraper by European stand-ards. From the top of it you can look down upon a harbor that seems brand new in its docks, wharves and other port equipment. And to tell the truth, a great deal of it is just that.

450 YEARS OF IMPORTANCE

Back in the year 1516, Le Havre was nothing but a fishing village and had been since Roman times. It received its name (Havre de Grace, in full) from a chapel which Francis I named Notre Dame de Grace. This same Francis appears to be the first to realize Le Havre's importance to sea trade, but before long it had become a naval base of great military importance. It had a turbulent history during the sixteenth and seventeenth centuries. The Prince of Conde, Louis I, delivered it to Queen Elizabeth for keeping, but shortly thereafter Charles IX expelled the English. His mother, the fierce old Catherine de Medici, personally took over the control of the city.

The many-sided Cardinal Richelieu continued harbor construction which Francis I had begun. Sebastian de Orestre de Vauban planned and executed the fortification. Intermittently from 1694 to 1795 Le Havre suffered bombardment by the English fleet, but despite military disruption, the port had flourished. It had become an important commercial seaport as early as 1572, when its fleet of whalers would put out for Spitzbergen and Newfoundland. It also became head-quarters for some great French colonizing and trading companies—the French East India Company and Senegal and Guinea Companies among them.

Napoleon I made Le Havre a war harbor of the first rank. Napoleon III completed certain harbor works programs started by Louis XVI. Then followed years of peace and prosperity. Le Havre became increasingly vital to world trade, especially to that of France. Imports, exports and Euporean travel all contributed their part to its continuing growth.

World War I brought a further boom. The Americans used Le Havre as a port of embarkation and debarkation. So did the British —as a great supply port. The Allies put it to use after the war as the particular embarkation port for returning soldiers. But it is only since the end of World War I that it has gained stature as a passenger seaport and a gateway for the importation of coffee, cotton and a score of other vital products. From the port of Le Havre also the great liner *Normandie,* of pathetic memory, started her record-breaking voyage to New York on May 29, 1935.

Since 1940, when the Germans pounded Le Havre and all her wharves and docking facilities into rubble, the new installations have made it one of the two or three most up-to-date seaports of the world. Le Havre residents remember, with a shudder, the time the Germans took over. They saw the invasion battles of Omaha and other beaches whose names have become milestones of history.

But not all the century-old charm of Le Havre and the Seine River estuary has departed. Stand on the docks and look across to the ancient port of Honfleur: It was powerful in the thirteenth century and has remained largely untouched by the wartime bombing. It is considered by experts the most picturesque coastal town of Normandie. Many tourists, however—especially we Americans—pass up Honfleur in their rush to Paris. But not the true artist, nor the scholar, nor the lover of ancient coastal architecture.

They call Le Havre the dinner basket of France. Even in the lean years, Normandie had it somewhat better than the rest of France. It is the paradise of the cow and the steamship—the one producing cheeses of worldwide reputation, the other bearing them away to all parts of the globe.

The teeming port of Marseilles, France.

MARSEILLES

W HEN France was hardly more than an assortment of warring tribes, Marseilles was already an important Mediterranean seaport. It was one of the outposts of the Phoenicians, another fishing village that became a center of trade.

97

Today that old port lies side by side with the new. The big ships lie along the great quays in the new harbor, while the old port is abustle with tiny craft of all kinds. Up from the colorful waterfront rises a labyrinth of steep, narrow and dark streets. Marseilles continues to fight a running battle with her neighbor, Genoa, for domination of the North Mediterranean trade. She plays hostess to the ships of the great lines that ply the routes to Africa, India, Indo-China, Australia and all the ports of the Mediterranean. Her docks are as busy as any from the Iberian Peninsula to the Red Sea.

Marseilles is the center of trade between France and the Far East. Imports include coal, copper, iron, machinery, metals, petroleum, coffee, cotton, hides, rice and sugar. Out of the port go the great wines of France, soap and cosmetics, olive oil, hides, tile and brick and hundreds of other commodities.

The fortunes of this ancient city have risen and fallen many times since the first Phoenician skippers dropped anchor in her harbor, but she remains one of the great seaports that seem to have an enduring capacity for survival.

BREST

THE fortified seaport of Brest lies at the westernmost tip of the Peninsula of Brittany; and Englishmen sometimes speak of it as the Land's End of France. It is, in fact, located in the Finistere district and is France's principal naval station. The harbor is considered one of the finest in Europe, connecting with the sea by only a narrow channel less than a mile in width, called Le Goulet.

The city itself rests on the north side of a magnificent land-locked bay, on the slopes of two hills divided by the River Penfeld. Not unlike the characteristics of other old fishing settlements along the French Atlantic coast, the hillsides to the east of the town along the river, which is the principal residential area, are so steep that ascent must be made by steps.

In the early days when England and France were almost continually at war there was a familiar saying "that he who is not lord of Brest is not Duke of Brittany."

The naval importance of the port has continued to develop since Richelieu, the port's great sponsor, in 1631 constructed a harbor of wooden wharves and fortified it. French naval activities including a large naval barracks now extend along both sides of the River Penfeld.

During World War I Brest harbor underwent tremendous expansion as it became the principal port of disembarkation for the American army fighting in France. Such heavy duty meant building large new docks and modernizing the olders ones.

In World War II it was occupied by Germany as a naval port after the French government surrendered in June, 1940. Two years later the Allies started consistently to bomb both town and harbor in an effort to wipe out submarine pens and open the way for the invasion of Brittany. The city and port fell to the Allies on September 20, 1944.

Although one of the finest harbors in the world Brest folk rarely see any of the world's great merchantmen. The proud men-of-war of France must be satisfied with glamorless coastal fishing boats and tramp steamers for civilian counterparts.

CHERBOURG

WE LANDED at Cherbourg."

For generations, numberless traveled Americans have thus begun the tales of their Grand Tours of the continent, and let it go at that. On landing, they rush pell mell to Paris, to Vienna, to Venice, to Naples, to Rome. But Cherbourg is a port of call that has infinite importance, variety, and invitation. It is a gateway to the garden provinces of Normandy.

Cherbourg first became important to French history as a naval station—a fortified channel port—in the fifteenth and sixteenth centuries, but it had been important in the relentless march of civilization's progress in Western Europe from prehistoric times. Excavations when the harbor and fortifications were built—and since—have unearthed relics which indicate that the site of Cherbourg was used by prehistoric traders as a base from which to voyage to the opposite side of the English Channel. The Romans used it also.

The centuries marched by. Great personages of history gave Cherbourg recognition. William the Conquerer built it a hospital and a church. Early English Kings—including Henry II—made their temporary residences there. Frequently it played a key role in the military aggressions which marked the struggle for power in Western Europe. Sometimes the port of Cherbourg fell under English rule, more often French. Elaborate fortifications were built by Vauban, the distinguished French military engineer. Shortly afterwards, however, these fortifications were dismantled and Cherbourg took an increasingly important part in the commercial development of France in the promotion of world trade and commerce.

The first harbor works were undertaken by Louis XVI and continued by Napoleon, Louis Philippe and Napoleon III. More than 8 million dollars were expended to make the port and harbors secure from channel storms. Two harbors were created, in part from rock formation. They lie at the mouth of the Divette River on a small bay, backed up by the steep Montagne du Roule. The harbors are formed on the outer tidal enclosure of about seventeen acres and the so-called river basin of sixteen acres. Beyond these lies the triangular bay which forms the roadstead of Cherbourg.

Cherbourg's outer bay thus lies in a natural shelter which protects it on three sides. On the fourth is the great seawall and breakwater begun by Louis XVI. In 1859 the first stages of the harbor and breakwater were completed. Eighteen eighty-nine saw the harbor further expanded and modernized.

This great breakwater incidentally is 650 feet at its base and 30 feet at the top. Many consider it a marvel of marine engineering. Within this "digne," dock the great transatlantic liners which have made Cherbourg synonymous with "port-of-entry" in the lexicon of world travelers. Through the port moves a variety of cargoes to supply France from her colonies and from other world nations. Cherbourg is a major importer of wine and oil. And it is from Cherbourg that

France exports stone and farm produce from the Normandy country-side to most other European maritime nations. Britain is Cherbourg's chief customer. Ships departing Cherbourg also send to markets of the world some of the products of its local industries—copper manufactured goods, rope, ships and boats, tanned hides, and fish. It is connected with the interior by the important Ouest Etat railway.

This port's proximity to the British Isles made it a vital locale both to the Germans and the Allies during World War II. It was heavily fortified and guarded by mine fields. Germans used the port for a submarine and a sea raider base and for military headquarters for the channel fortification along the beaches.

Again and again British and American bombers dropped their fearful eggs during the German occupation. A great many of its historic buildings and homes were blasted out of existence. A number of its patriotic citizens (non-collaboratists) fell victim to the Germans, both as hostages and as participants in the French underground movement.

Finally after the great invasions via the Normandy coast, the Cotintin Peninsula fell to the Allies. Cherbourg then became the major port of supply for the forces which were to sweep to the Rhine and to ultimate victory in Europe. Four pipelines were laid between the Isle of Wight and Cherbourg which provided a continuous flow of petroleum for the European forces—beginning ten hours after the seas had been swept of mines.

In those stirring but dreadful days, the port of Cherbourg was visited by perhaps more ships than the total sum arriving there in the ten preceding decades. Ships of every type they were—studding the harbors, the roadstead and beyond, waiting for entry in the channel. But ships did not wait to berth in order to unload. The busy Army "ducks" plowed through choppy seas to take supplies from the ships and land them wherever a hardstand on the beaches could be arranged.

After the war the port of Cherbourg metamorphosed into a mercy port. Through it moved the incredible amount of supplies needed to save France from starvation and to rehabilitate the shattered economic and industrial life of the hardest hit Ally. Since the port was then without electrical power, the ships simply docked and turned their engines into generating plants.

In the late 1940's and through the 1950's, a building boom has brought Cherbourg out of the rubble, into the normal course of serving once again as a gateway to Europe. It also serves as the open door to the promised land of plenty, which has been Normandy's role through the centuries.

COBH

W HEN you arrive at Cobh, Ireland—actually on an island—you disbark in a harbor which is four miles long and could shelter the whole British fleet.

Most passengers show little interest in the city of Cobh and anxiously wait for their boat train to carry them the fifteen-odd miles to perhaps the most appealing city in Ireland—Cork.

Cobh itself, however, is a quaint old world place. It has pastel-painted houses and inns facing the harbor. Narrow streets climb a hill crowned by a large cathedral.

The city first attracted attention when England used it as a base in the eighteenth century war with France, of which the American Revolution proved to be a most important part.

It was from Cobh that the *Sirius*, first steamer ever to make the voyage from Europe to America, sailed in 1836. It was also from Cobh that Queen Victoria first set foot on Irish soil. In her honor the name of Cobh gave way to "Queenstown." During the famine years, many Irish people emigrated to the states from Queenstown. With the passing of English rule in the Old Green Isle, the port became Cobh again.

ANTWERP

To the reader of maritime history the Port of Antwerp is primarily the ancient seat of the Hanseatic League, the home of great artists—Rubens and Van Dyke—and of diamond cutters whose skill has gone round the world.

But Antwerp thinks of herself first of all as the third largest seaport in the world. As your ship approaches the city, she goes plowing up the Scheldt past mile after mile of wharves with world shipping berthed stern-first or bow-on, clearing or entering the port. Soon you find your thinking has joined that of the good people of the town. An American traveler feels a sense of kinship with this ancient seaport as he sees from the steamer deck the names of great industrial plants of his homeland—General Motors and Ford among them.

The quays in their very names smack of both the present and the past. You see, berthed alongside Quai Ortelius, Quai Jordaens, Quai Van Dyck and Quai Plantin, modern passenger and freight liners flying the house flags of every major shipping company in the world.

More than likely as you pass Steen Castle, you recall that it was here the Spanish Inquisition got in some of its bloodiest work. The castle, even in those earlier days of religious conflict, was six centuries old. It stands there, at the entering-in of Antwerp, on the fortress site of a defense work built by the tyrant Antigonus.

This monarch levied tolls on all merchant ships entering the Scheldt—tolls that for size would stack up well with anything American businessmen have to pay today. Did a certain bold skipper refuse to pay the toll? Antigonus took him in, cut off that skipper's right hand, and turned him loose. One skipper, however (since become a hero), proved recalcitrant beyond most of his fellow seamen and in the ensuing carnage cut off the right hand of Antigonus and threw it into the Scheldt. That, claim the people of Antwerp, gave the town its name—a corruption of *Hand Werper*.

It would be hard to find any harbor offering a more impressive sight to the first-time visitor than Antwerp. The first things that catch your eye as you approach the city are two towers rising above all other buildings. From whatever point you look, you can see them sharp against the sky—the heaven-kissing cathedral spire and the equally soaring, but less inspiring, tower of the twenty-four story Farmers Bank Building. Belgian King Charles V did not see the bank building, but he did study the cathedral tower and compared it gracefully to Malines lace. The bank tower expresses the industrial fabric of Antwerp. And both bank and cathedral emphasize the air of paradox—old versus new—that seems to pervade this mighty port.

A stranger, commenting on the present vastness of Antwerp's maritime activities, was told that in the heyday of the Hansa merchants, under Charles V, five hundred ships sometimes entered the port between two sun-ups. What a sight they must have been! Venetian galleys. Genoese caracks. Spanish caravels. A galleon or two! Sails of all colors! Merchandise of every description.

Such prosperity in the old Belgian metropolis aroused the enmity of the Dutch who controlled the mouth of the Scheldt. In 1648, therefore, they contrived to choke off most of the commerce headed by ship to Antwerp.

The French, during the first Napoleonic regime, reopened the river, spent millions of dollars on its development. After Waterloo a mighty prosperity swept over Belgium, centering at Antwerp, and except for continuing disputes with the Dutch on the right to levy dues on shipping, prosperity has continued ever since. Not even two world wars have been able to prevent its growth.

HAMBURG

Hamburg's harbor has a British look. The gaunt frames of giant cranes stand out stark above the low-lying landscape. Squat stacks of the big ocean liners—Hamburg-American, Cunard and others—rise steeply from the walls. While hulls of the Peninsula-Oriental ships show up sharply against the sweep of weather-beaten warehouses. Tugs scurry about like overgrown waterbugs, piercing the clatter of sound with their steam-throated signals. Hundreds of barges go pushing their way up and down the channel, bearing world cargoes ranging from sugar to guano, from hydraulic machinery to sewing-machines and bicycles.

Hamburg is said to be the largest continental seaport in Europe. It has been an important harbor since the days of the Hanseatic League, but only within the past hundred years has it come fully into its own as a vast transit and distribution center for the entire continent.

Because ships bearing coffee from South America by the thousands of tons come up the Elbe, Hamburg is known as "the coffee-pot of Europe." The Middle East and America send cargoes of tobacco; the Orient, tea, spices, sugar, cereals, rice, hemp, jute. Coal comes from England and America.

Down the river from Hamburg and out to sea go dairy products, iron and steel in many forms, china and glassware, electrical goods, motor cars, cocoa and some of the world's finest beer.

Shipbuilding is one of Hamburg's chief industries today. From her extensive shipyards come great freighters and passenger ships, even as they came a half century ago.

Boys watch the giant ships in the harbor at Hamburg, Germany.

More ships at Hamburg.

ARBEITSGEMEINSCHAFT FUR WIRTSCHAFTSFORDERUNG E. V.

Hanseatic League. Merchants dispatching their goods in a Medieval harbor.

106

Hanseatic League

Hamburg was a flourishing town in the year 1241 when her merchants made a defense pact with the city of Luebeck, one of the most important of agreements in the development of the historic Hanseatic League formed for mutual defense and prosperity. The word Hanse in early German society meant simply an organization of men; the units making up the league were actually started by German merchants in Baltic ports and in London, their chief aim being to protect their own trading interests.

Later merchants in the cities in Germany followed suit and set up additional *Hanses* to protect and coordinate their commerce with other ports. In its heyday the Hanseatic League included seaports from Dordrecht on the North Sea, up the Baltic to the Russian city of Nizhni Novgorod. In it were the ports of Bremen, Hamburg, Luebeck, Stettin, Danzig, Elbing, Konigsburg, Riga and Reval. Inland towns having mercantile connections with the seaports included Cologne, Munster, Dortmund, Brunswick, Magdeburg, Soest and Prague: they too had their "Hanses."

In the early days of the Hanseatic merchants, the cities of Western Europe traded cloth, metals, wine, beer and other manufactured goods for the raw products of the Scandinavian countries—"naval stores," pitch, tar and turpentine, as well as fish, timber and tallow for the candles of the homes and churches. Another major product was furs, almost a life-and-death item to central Germany, for the homes of Europe were cold as the tomb. The problem was serious enough in those days to cause a German bishop to say, "We strive as hard to come into the possession of a marten skin as if it were everlasting salvation."

Merchants, as well as their goods, were considered legitimate booty for anybody. There was no central, no national military government to protect them. Like the great free cities of the Mediterranean—Tyre, Sidon, Alexandria, Carthage, Venice, Rome, Genoa—each acted alone. But the cities of the North seem to have been the first to develop trade alliances involving groups of merchants in several ports and inland trade centers. All united for profit.

Meanwhile, the Germanic nobility were beginning to feel the blight of decline due to the League's growing mercantile power. Ignorant, untrained for anything useful, the nobility were too proud to do anything about it. The merchants educated themselves and their children, learned how to keep accounts, how to read a little Latin and German, how to speak two or three languages. Some of them had actually been knighted. Some even had the presumption, in the eyes of the landed gentry, to create their own coats of arms!

But warfare was the only thing the nobles and the gentry knew and they weren't very good at that, as the little incident known as the Hare War demonstrated. Toward the end of the thirteenth century, the knights of the noble family of Holstein began to resent their merchant neighbors in Dietmarsh, downriver from Hamburg. So they assembled an army and marched toward the town. As they neared the enemy, the troops in front saw a hare go leaping across the road. Someone shouted, "Run, Run!"

The soldiers behind took up the cry. The troops to *their* rear thought somebody was giving them a warning of danger and they too began to run for dear life. Next the troops in front looked behind and saw their comrades disappearing down the road and across the fields. Believing that the troops behind had scented danger, they turned and scurried after them.

About this time, the Dietmarsh army came along the road, saw the well-planned withdrawal of the nobles and decided to turn the occasion into a massacre.

More than once the nobility banded together and descended on the towns, slaughtering merchants and making off with their goods. So the towns in turn banded together and struck back. In 1352 Hamburg and Luebeck put together an army of 2,500 men to punish the nobles. They destroyed several castles and hanged some of the nobility.

Pirates and freebooters roved the North Sea as they did most other waters in those days. The most famous of all these sea rovers of the North was Klaus Stortebacher, said to be a nobleman from Verden, who had spent his inheritance in riotous living and then had taken to the open sea.

Up and down the rivers and seaways from port to port old Storte and his gang went—doing damage to the merchants of Hamburg, destroying ships, interfering with trade. In 1402, an expedition was organized to retaliate. Stortebacher and his brethren were anchored at the mouth of the Elbe, where they waylaid all ships coming from or going toward Hamburg.

The avenging fleet, under the command of a young man named Simon von Utrecht, came ranging in. The night before the attack was planned, a pilot, Peter Krutzfeldt, had been sent on a spying expedition downriver to the mouth of the Elbe. There he was put over the side in a small boat. In the darkness, he rowed out to the flagship of old Stortebacher—it was called the *Mad Dog*—and jimmied the rudder.

Next morning, Commander von Utrecht and his fleet moved down the Elbe, the commander leading in his flagship, *Brindled Cow*.

At first, the pirates thought the approaching fleet was a rich merchant prize. Then as the big *Brindled Cow* came directly for the *Mad Dog*, Stortebacher saw he was in for a fight. A pirate captain, seeing his leader's ship was not responding to its helm, sailed in toward the *Brindled Cow* and fired a broadside. Von Utrecht charged the interfering ship bow-on and rammed it, crippling it completely. Then he lay alongside the *Mad Dog*, grappled and boarded her.

Von Utrecht sought out Stortebacher and fought a hand-to-hand battle. They slashed at each other with swords and axes until the swords were shattered and the axes slid from their sweaty hands. They grappled together, trying to do with their bare hands what they had been unable to do with steel.

Stortebacher, a giant of a man, had an edge in weight and strength and these began to tell. Von Utrecht was thrown to the deck of the ship. But at that moment, two stout Hamburgers leaped upon the pirate, overpowered him and bound him hand and foot. At this point the desperadoes began to lose interest in the engagement. Several of their ships, with crews and captains, had been captured. The others made off across the water.

When young von Utrecht returned to Hamburg with his trussed-up prisoner, the people of the city went wild with joy. Stortebacher, terror of the seas, stood helpless before them. But although the townspeople beheaded him on the spot, the end was not yet. A few weeks later, Simon von Utrecht ran down about eighty more of the freebooter brethren and brought them back to Hamburg for execution. One of them was said to be a man by the name of Wigbolt, a scholar and Master of Philosophy from the University of Rostock!

Simon von Utrecht became honorary burgomaster of the great port of Hamburg.

BREMEN

Wıᴛʜ Hamburg, Bremen shares the honor of upholding the great traditions of the Hanseatic cities. Today, Bremen, forty-six miles up the Weser River from the North Sea, is Germany's second greatest port. Like Hamburg, most of her trade is transit. Great quantities of American products enter the harbor for shipment throughout Europe. Correspondingly huge exports of great diversity move out to sea from Bremen's docks.

In the winding streets of the old town, the massive gabled houses of the Hanseatic days still stand in rugged dignity, reminders of the solid character and the achievements of the men who built them in the days when the sea merchants matched wits and muscle with their enemies.

LUEBECK

Tʜᴇ sheltered harbor of Luebeck, on the River Trave, dominated the sea trade of the Baltic during the early years of the Hanseatic League. Although it was gradually superseded by Hamburg, Bremen and Stetin, the city still conducts a busy trade in the Baltic, importing coal, grain, timber, steel and copper. She exports manufactured goods, minerals and other products.

The decline of Luebeck followed the demise of the Hanseatic League. In her early prosperity, the town had done a thriving trade in herring fishery, but as shipping activity increased, the herring were driven away.

In the early days of the League, the German merchants established branch offices in the seaports all about them, in England and in the Scandinavian countries. Through their extensive organization, they cornered much of the commerce that would have gone to local merchants. They made monopolistic trade agreements with other countries to protect their League. The League cities waxed powerful and rich, so that at the height of her glory, Luebeck was shipping its merchandise throughout all North Europe.

Sir Thomas Gresham, who became the presiding financial genius for Queen Elizabeth, cut his trade teeth with the Hanseatic merchants. He had watched and admired the growth of their enterprise. But when the threat to English commerce became too dangerous, he led the attack against the "Easterlings" (so the Germans were called) to break their stranglehold.

The British began to expand their trade rapidly. They followed the trade routes of the Portuguese and Spanish, and developed more of their own.

In Germany, the warring nobles were still fighting. There was little effort to form a unified government. But in England, the old wounds of feudal strife were healing, and the ancient hatreds were being transmuted into excitement over exploration and colonization.

The Hanseatic League was falling apart both from inner stress and foreign attack. The last official "diet" of the merchants of the Hanse of North Europe was held in 1630.

The Dutch

As the Hanse cities began to decline, Amsterdam and the whole of the Netherlands began their rise to greater prosperity. The Portuguese and the Spanish were busy developing trade and building up colonies in the Far East. The spice trade had become a gold rush. The cornucopia of South America poured its riches into the ports of Spain. The Iberian Peninsula flamed with the fever of empire.

The empire builders needed money, men and ships—and the Dutch had all three. By 1625, more than 16,000 seagoing vessels manned by 160,000 Dutch seamen flew the flags of the Netherlands.

Sir Walter Raleigh once said with considerable annoyance, "The Low-Countreys have as many ships and vessels as eleven kingdomes of Christendome have . . . and build every year neer one thousand ships, and not a timber tree growing in their own countrie."

At first, the Dutch ships merely carried cargoes for their Spanish and Portuguese partners. But the restless Iberians were new to the business of developing trade and managing colonies. They didn't care for the drudgery that went along with the adventure. After the first easy pickings, they began to lose interest. Here the industrious Dutch began to pick up the loose ends, their capacity for hard work and perseverance soon beginning to prove profitable.

For a while the Dutch merchants and traders made a free-for-all out of their individual efforts to grab a piece of business in the Orient. But their native good sense got the upper hand in time and they combined their interests in the Dutch East India Company.

The loss of ships and life in the 9000-mile Eastern trade was enormous, but the Dutch wouldn't give up. They built stronger ships and doubled their crews, hoping that at least half of the men would survive each trip. Finally, someone got the idea that there should be a break on the route to India, and thus was first established Capetown, on the southern tip of Africa.

Sometimes the Dutch made the same mistakes they had scorned in their Spanish and Portuguese friends. They tried to live by European standards in the Orient. For a time, they tried to plant their religious beliefs among the natives, but Calvinism, they found, just wasn't suited to the tropics.

The Dutch East India Company came into being in 1602 to further develop trade in the Orient. It established a firm foothold in the rich Malay states, the Spice Islands and Java. In that area the company slowly but firmly broke the power of the Portuguese. From these lush lands, some of the costliest luxuries of the day poured back into Amsterdam. The cargo of a single fleet of seven ships—bearing cinnamon, nutmeg, pepper and mace, indigo, shellac, raw silk, cotton textiles—rolled up several million dollars in profit to the owners.

There was a Dutch West India Company, too, but it was a little different from most of the usual colonial trading organizations. It was a fine auxiliary of Dutch national defense. Instead of making its profits from trade and colonial development, the company's most important source of income derived from the capture of Spanish ships bound from South America with rich cargoes of silver.

Because the Dutch put up so valiant a battle to win their independence from the powerful Spaniards, they became known as a people who have high regard for freedom and the rights of the individual. In one particular way they proved it. Some of their neighbors, in the sixteenth century, were flabbergasted at the freedom Dutch women enjoyed. "Dutch women manage all domestic affairs without their husbands' control," an Italian envoy reported with raised eyebrows. And the German artist, Albrecht Dürer, was set back on his haunches when he found that he was expected to bring his wife to a banquet held in his honor. Women even took part in politics and held public office.

Yet this appreciation of the value of personal freedom was misapplied in the commercial enterprises of the Dutch, who fought hard for free trade but neglected to join hands to protect their gains. In fact, they had the same weakness of division as the cities of the Hanseatic League—they had the idea of unity, without actual union; the shadow but not the substance.

Dutch commerce with the Orient increased until about the middle of the eighteenth century, but the country was still dependent for its sea power upon the strength of several ruling families. There was no central government. The Dutch managed their colonial possessions through private companies under charter, clutching bulging purses in their chubby hands. They kept all the fat jobs for themselves, padding payrolls with relatives instead of hiring outsiders who had the skills they needed. Instead of building up their colonies and expanding trade, they sat tight defending the *status quo* with all their might.

Gradually, the power of the Netherlands—the un-united Netherlands—began to play out. As inexorably as the Dutch took over from Portugal and Spain, Britain took over from the Dutch.

Vikings

I

N A small Norwegian valley that falls gently to the sea, a Viking ship-grave was unearthed near the village of Oseberg in 1903. The proud vessel lay beneath a mound of earth, anchored to a great stone, with its prow toward the sea, a monument to the Viking custom of burying chieftains with their ships.

Other Viking ship-graves had been discovered, but the Oseberg ship brought a shattering blow to tradition. In the burial chamber, generally reserved for the remains of a King, the skeletons of two *women* were found. The scholars scurried to their books and soon came back with the revelation that the two women must have been the great Queen Asa and her old bondswoman.

The Oseberg ship, moreover, was different from the rugged, seaworthy crafts that once spread terror through the sea villages of the North. It was a pleasure craft, designed for cruising in the protected waters of the fjords. It was broad and spacious, with fifteen oars on a side. The prow rose in a graceful, swan-like curve of richly carved timber.

In the great Marine Museum at Oslo, there are three fine examples of ancient Viking ships, with their sweeping lines and sturdy, strong hulls. The Vikings preserved their ships' timbers with thick coatings of pitch and caulked them with animal hair. At the bow the similitude of a fearsome dragon reared its head. At the stern the dragon's tail curved up over the rudder. Such ships, each propelled by a single sail, two score pairs of oarsmen working the flashing blades, and loaded with fighting men, roved the rough waters of the North Sea, landing upon many a shore distant from the Viking homeland.

Until the close of the eighth century, the Norse were not very well known to the rest of the world. They were busy making a living from the sea. They grew what crops they could and fought among themselves. But about the start of the ninth century, the phrase "Viking raid" became a household term of terror in every tongue from the British Isles to the steppes of Russia. When the swift ships with the square sails appeared on the horizon, villagers fell to their knees and prayed:

"Oh, Lord, deliver us from the rage of the Norsemen."

The term "viking" seems to have started with the Norwegians; it was later picked up, assumed and justified by the Danes and Swedes. It means "great seafaring warrior." To be a "viking" was the greatest ambition of every young man of the Scandinavian countries in those days. They were the sea-going knights of the North.

The first viking raids were experimental jaunts made by local boys out for a bit of adventure. But after a few of them returned with cargoes of booty from an unprotected monastery or an unwary village, the commercial aspects of sea-raiding began to appear more and more enticing. It wasn't long before the enterprising Norwegians, Danes and Swedes were organizing expeditions right and left.

In 843, the Norwegians attacked the guarded city of Nantes, in France, with a fleet of about seventy ships and fortified the Island of Moirmoutier in the Loire estuary as a base for future raids. A few years later, they roved southward to Spain and into the Mediterranean.

Both the Norwegians and the Danes established settlements in England. In 867, the Danes captured York and established a base of operations. Their neighbors, the Norwegians, fought beside them against the stubborn Britons. But when the Anglo-Saxon King Alfred took out after the invaders, he made short shrift of these attacks. The commandos from the North were no match for the great Alfred. He beat the pagans soundly, captured their King and baptized him into Christianity, willy-nilly, along with twenty-nine of his followers.

Through their pillaging proclivities, however, the vikings pioneered the new sea trails from the Continent to England which became in time the paths of sea commerce.

In the old Icelandic sagas there are obscure references to the distant shores of "Wineland the Good." According to some sources, the first Norseman to sight "Wineland the Good" (the North American continent) was Bjorne Herjolfsson. His ship became lost in a great

OSLO

For all of its viking heritage, the seaport of Oslo is best remembered by many who visit it for the beauty of the wooded hills that rise above it, for the richness of its culture, for the hearty happiness of the people.

The shouts of the vikings are now replaced by the hoots of busy trawlers and deep-throated steamers in Oslo harbor. Oslo is the major port of Norway, a country that imports about three times as much as it exports.

STOCKHOLM

ACCORDING to the *Erik Chronicle* of the fourteenth century, Stockholm was founded by Birger Jarl.

All cities have their special names, but Stockholm seems to have more than most. For hundreds of years this Swedish capital has been referred to as "The Venice of the North," because of the multitudes of islands with canal-like channels between them. She has other

Stockholm, Sweden, c. 1850.

names too: "City of Lights and Waters," "City of Space and Grace," "City Between the Bridges." She further claims the title of "Diplomatic City," for there are seven embassies in Stockholm, forty-five ministries and seventeen consulates general, housing about two hundred and sixty diplomatic representatives from other countries who reside pleasantly there.

M/S Kungsholm, the Swedish American Line, arriving at Gothenburg.

GOTHENBURG

ON THE other side of the Swedish peninsula lies the port of Gothenburg, largest oil harbor in all Scandinavia. Gothenburg's municipal life is centered about this great harbor. The tides are slight. Ships can berth at the quays any time of the day or night. Railways and roads from all over Sweden lead to Gothenburg which is linked to the great inland lakes by the Göta Canal.

The Gothenburg Fish Harbor, opened nearly half a century ago, is the biggest fish market in Scandinavia. Shipbuilding, too, is a major industry. About 400,000 tons come down the launching ways every year from the shipyards in the harbor.

COPENHAGEN

C OPENHAGEN, capital city of Denmark, lies on the island of Zealand, just off the lower tip of Sweden. In 1958, the Port of Copenhagen Authority celebrated its one hundredth anniversary with the publication of a special issue of the *Harbor Journal*. Even through the modest enthusiasm of the Danes for their capital port shines the sense of vitality of a sea-loving race that still makes Copenhagen one of the busiest and most interesting centers of world sea-trade.

Copenhagen is another of those natural deep-water ports with no tide—so favorable to the cargo vessels that arrive all hours of the day and night from all the ports of the world.

Like so many seaports, Denmark's capital city was first a fishing village. A few years before the beginning of the thirteenth century, the local squire built fortifications to defend his people against the pirates.

Copenhagen thrived on the unstable conditions in Europe by remaining a neutral city during the seventeenth and eighteenth centuries. Merchants from other countries preferred to trade in Copenhagen, where they could be more certain their goods wouldn't be confiscated in the overthrow of the government.

Modern Copenhagen is, like her sister cities of the North, a blend of the old and the new. There are still narrow cobblestone streets lined with quaint gabled houses. But near by are sleek, modern apartments or office buildings reaching up above their neighbors. And everywhere you turn there are bright, gay, open-air flower markets.

One of the photographs in the anniversary issue of the *Harbor Journal* shows the bridge at Knippelsbro in the year 1860 with sailing vessels lined up on either side. Hundreds of sailboats appear in Copenhagen port to this day—big and little fishing boats among the freighters and passenger liners from all over the world.

121

Some Major People from Minor Ports

MANY of Europe's smaller seaports owe their place in history to the exploits of a single individual, without whose attractive personality or acts of daring they might have remained virtually unheard of.

Palos, of course, is one of these; its name is inscribed on the pages of mankind's story book only because Christopher Columbus sailed from its shores to blaze a new sea trail and change the course of western history.

It was a thirteenth century romance and ensuing tragedy, for example, that brought to Bristol, ninety miles west of London, its first own measure of historic fame. Robert Macham was the man who accomplished this, with the connivance and loyalty of a lovely lady.

Macham was a gentleman well known in the West Country, a man of parts, certainly of pronounced courage and apparently extremely attractive. He fell violently in love with a pretty neighbor of his, and although she had a perfectly good husband at the time, she responded with enthusiasm.

The two decided to elope to some foreign strand and found a colony, a lover's paradise. France, they knew, welcomed such lovers on the loose. So Macham came up to London and hired a sturdy little ship in which to transport his lady love together with supplies and all the essentials for founding a colony. They sailed from Bristol, rounded Land's End and Lizard Point, headed straight towards the continent beyond the English Channel.

But crossing that wild and stormy water in those days was not the mere hour-and-a-half ferry ride that it is today. And in addition, their water-borne journey before they reached the Channel had already been a good stiff one.

122

No sooner had the ship struck into the open North Atlantic than the unpredictable sea rose in her wrath, as though to register her disapproval of the illicit though undeniably devoted enterprise. The rains descended. The winds came. The big seas rolled up. The ship strained and creaked.

Macham and his crew battled the seas for fourteen days. And the lady stayed right by him, brave in her determination to find a haven for their romance. France? . . . they lost all track of direction and finally gave it up, to make an effort to beat back up to the shore of England. The contrary winds persisting, they were swept southward toward the coast of the Iberian peninsula. There, the little ship piled up on what later came to be known as the Island of Madeira, off the coast of Portugal.

Madeira would have been an excellent place in which to romance, but Macham and his lady never realized their dream. They died amid the wreckage of their ship. A sailor or two returned to bring back the intelligence to London of the first would-be settler on the shores of Madeira.

Hardly had Macham's name ceased to circulate through maritime England than people were reading the exciting exploits of one Sir John Mandeville. Sir John recorded in his volumes that he had set sail on Michaelmas Day, 1322, to circumnavigate the globe and that he had done just that—many years before Magellan accomplished the trick!

Mandeville wrote with great color and reality. His knowledge of ships and his nautical terminology were pronounced fine. Moreover he wrote with a conviction-carrying zest that readers loved in those days even as they do today. Had he lived today he would have been called a science fiction writer with a strong emphasis on the fiction. He knew the shape of the earth. He knew how to sail by a fix on the North Star. But "Sir John," alas, proved to be only a discredited physician of Liège, France, who had come to England to escape the shackles of the law in his own country.

Local records contradicted just about everything "Sir John" had written as to his personal history and his birthplace. Before long, even in those days when news moved at a snail's pace, word of the hoax got around. No record exists to show what crime Mandeville had been guilty of. In any case, an interesting production of an author's imagination went down before the cold tyranny of facts.

Late in the 1480's one Giovanni Caboto, lately a merchant of Venice, showed up in England. For whatever reasons, he changed his name to John Cabot. Those were the days when there was quite a sizable colony of these Italian merchant mariners in London. Although it would be too much to say they taught England her love for ships and the sea, they were instrumental in intensifying that love; the red-and-gold sails of Italian ships lent much color to London's old gray port.

Cabot, before long, had caught the London disease then epidemic along the Thames—the urge to sail and seek that illusive westward passage to Asia. He had heard of two ships that set sail out of Bristol in July 1480 bound for "the island of Brazil," though with questionable accomplishments. Cabot believed he could find the island that was thought to stand between England and the Far East, and he convinced some London merchants that it would be to their decided advantage to finance his explorations. Year after year, Cabot took small fleets of ships out into the western ocean, disappearing over the horizon. Year after year Cabot returned, coming back up over the horizon to Bristol, or sometimes to London, without having sighted the island he continuously sought.

Then in 1493 came news that a fellow Italian had made a successful voyage to some island in the general vicinity of the land which Cabot supposed he sought. This Genoese was named Christopher Columbus, and at once, merchants in the heart of London Port, in Bristol, and in other shipping centers, fell victims to the fever. The flame of discovery waxed hot and roared high once more. Cabot made another try at it, having induced some Bristol merchants to forget the money thus far invested in his ventures. Although without tangible returns, the merchants listened once more. Once again, they came up with the needed sum.

Away sailed Cabot into the sunset, his red sails glowing. And back came Cabot once again with a report which, try as he would to make it sound optimistic, could be summed up only in this way: "No results."

Despite these continued failures, March 5, 1496, found Cabot proudly displaying a letter of patent from Henry VII, giving to his ". . . well beloved John Cabot, sometime citizen of Venice, to

Lewis, Sebastian, and Santius, sonnes of the said John . . . leave and power to saile to all parts, countries, and seas of the East, of the West, and of the North, under our banners and ensigns, with five shippes . . ."

The contract further provided: "All the fruits, profits, gaines and commodities growing out of such navigation" could enter the Port of Bristol free of customs. And too, that "not a single person could visit the newly discovered land without the license of the foresayd John and his sonnes."

So John Cabot and his "sonnes" got themselves a trade monopoly blessed by Royal decree and while they were gloating over this prize, news came that Christopher Columbus had returned from a second voyage to the New World with samples of rare merchandise plus some good, hard negotiable gold.

Once again the merchants of Bristol loosened their purse strings. But not even a royal charter could bring John Cabot the "five shippes" he wanted. He set sail in one small ship, with a crew said to include only eighteen men, which may have included two of his three sons.

The rest of Cabot's story is recorded history. He planted the flag of England on the "new found land." It was inhabited, he was sure, for there were notched trees and snares for small animals.

John Cabot thought he had landed on the shores of Asia. When he returned to London to announce his discovery to King Henry, the monarch was so pleased that he issued another royal charter to the explorer and even invested some of his own funds in the new expedition, which was sure—he thought—to bring back great cargoes of spices, silks, rare gems and other Eastern treasures.

But Cabot returned from this expedition with empty ships and no fresh promise of riches. He was through as an explorer.

Of all the brilliant seafaring men who surrounded Elizabeth I one of the most intriguing was Sir John Hawkins, a tough customer and sometimes ruthless. Yet none deserves more credit for the victory over the Spanish Armada than he. Jack Hawkins lacked the attractive personality, the gracious manner of the courtier. Indeed he seems to have had uncommon ability to say the wrong thing at the right time. But there was one thing he could do with incomparable skill. He could design and build ships to a Queen's taste!

He grew up in the waters of Plymouth Harbor. Hawkins knew every plank of his ships, every spar, every line, from truck to keelson. His men trusted him as their commander; his officers respected him because of his knowledge of ships and the sea.

Blunt, tough Jack Hawkins! He never learned to "make a good impression." His forthright honesty of speech often made enemies of those whose friendship he needed. His own account of the battle with the Armada, written as he says "in haste and bad weather," leaves much to be desired. For one thing, it makes little mention of his own magnificent leadership. For another, it does not describe in full detail the combat advantages of the English ships—designed by Hawkins himself—over those of Spain.

When Hawkins was not out fighting or sailing the seas he was designing more ships—foreshadowing the shape of ships to come: surely one of his greatest contributions to his country and to international trade. Hawkins apparently was the first to understand fully that the best way to beat the powerful Spanish vessels, with their "castles" and their slow and ponderous movement and heavy cargoes, was to design ships of smaller size but greater maneuverability. Hawkins built craft that did away with the old high bulwarks, the tall and topheavy upper works, fore and aft.

"Revolutionary!" some old sea dogs snarled, just as later intransigents were to deride steam vessels and iron hulls. It took some time to convince Elizabeth herself of the value of Hawkins' ships. Not until definite news came that the Spanish invasion was impending, did the headstrong Queen give her full support to the ships from the Hawkins' yard. But once she gave it, Hawkins did wonders.

One of England's most renowned seafaring heroes has lent the aura of greatness to his native town, the small Devonshire community of Tavistock.

For here was born in 1540—not far from the Plymouth home of his kinsman, Jack Hawkins—one Francis Drake. Before reaching the age of forty, he was destined to be the first man to carry the flag of England around the world.

England lagged behind other nations in the exploration of new lands and the establishment of colonies for many years after the discoveries of Cabot. The Portuguese had reached India, the East Indies and Japan. The Spanish had established colonies throughout

South America and the East. Hawkins and Drake were content for a time to follow in the tracks of the Portuguese and Spanish, plundering ships and settlements. On a voyage along the African coast in 1567, more than twenty years before the battle of the Armada, the Spaniards caught up with these two Englishmen and beat them brutally.

For this, Drake and Hawkins vowed vengeance on the Spaniards. Drake made good his vow in a spectacular raid on the Spanish Main. The Spanish had a monopoly of trade and colonization in South America, carrying fabulous cargoes along the West Coast of South America up to the Isthmus of Panama, where the riches were carried overland to be shipped home over the Atlantic. With no one to molest their Pacific route to Panama, the Spanish treasure ships were going unescorted and virtually unarmed.

Drake set sail for the Caribbean with two small ships, the *Pasha* and the *Swan*. He plundered ships and towns wherever the pickings looked ripe. The little Spanish town of Nombre de Dios was perhaps the ripest. When Drake's men entered the storehouse of the governor, it is said that they saw a pile of silver bars stacked one on the other to a height of twelve feet, a breadth of ten feet, and seventy feet in length. This heap of wealth was referred to as "no more than ballast, compared with the store of gold and jewels that was taken."

But raging fevers swept through the ranks of Drake's men. About half the number who set out from England died. His brother, John, was among them. The great seaman, however, returned home with a cargo of riches more fabulous than any adventurer had dreamed of. Accounts of Drake's entry into Plymouth harbor on Sunday, August 9, 1573, say that the guns of the port roared a welcome, and that when the salute was returned by the homecoming ship, the townspeople rose up from their pews in the town church and left their minister gaping in dismay as they hurried to the waterfront to greet their great townsman.

It was on this voyage that Drake became the first Englishman to sight the Pacific Ocean. It seems a little ridiculous that so great a sailor should have had to shinny up a tree for his first look at the Pacific. But it's history!

The Spanish were mad as hornets over what they called the

raids of the "pirate, Drake." They protested bitterly. But Elizabeth was becoming more and more vexed with the efforts of Philip of Spain to damage English sea trade and cripple England as a world power. When Drake proposed another raid on the Spanish treasures of South America, she gave her consent and support.

There was a special element of daring to Drake's new proposal. He would take a fleet of ships through the fierce Straits of Magellan.

It had been more than fifty years since Magellan had successfully negotiated the lower tip of the American continents. In the meantime, many others had tried. Most had met disaster. Cortez, Sebastian Cabot and Amerigo Vespucci were among those who failed. Sailors began to have such a horror of the Straits that they refused to take a ship into them. One explorer, Simon of Alcozova, was murdered by his men when he insisted on taking his ship into those ill-fated waters.

Drake left England in December 1577 with of fleet of five ships. Ahead of him lay the most eventful voyage of his career: a voyage in which he would encounter a plot to incite mutiny; the mysteries of black magic; greater riches than ever before; and the provocation of war with Spain.

The mutiny was instigated by Thomas Doughty, friend and shipmate of Drake. It was discovered early and Doughty was given a trial. He was found guilty by a jury of forty members of the company, and was executed.

There were some indications that Doughty had been influenced by the Spanish, that he might even have been paid to instigate mutiny and take control of the voyage. In any event, his followers were not subdued by the execution, and the incident continued to shadow Drake for many years. Doughty's principal sponsor was Christopher Hatton, a member of the Queen's Privy Council and her newest favorite. Perhaps it was in order to make amends to Hatton that Drake re-christened his flagship *The Golden Hind*, since Hatton's crest bore the figure of a hind.

The black magic seems to have made its first appearance when the little fleet anchored somewhere near the mouth of the Rio Grande. The crews were rejoicing at the prospect of fresh water and a chance to clean their ships when the happy weather was suddenly turned to blackest night by a dense fog. A quick storm separated the ships. Then suddenly, both storm and fog were gone. But so was one of the ships.

The pilot explained that they were off what the Portuguese seamen called *Terra Demonum*—Demonland. He said that the natives had been tortured by white men who invaded their land. In order to protect themselves from other raids, the people came down to the shore when ships approached, threw a cloud of sand into the air and invoked their gods to defend them. When the gods were amenable, they sent the fog and storms to aid their worshippers.

Of the five ships that set out from England to pass through the Straits of Magellan, only the newly christened *Golden Hind* got through. The others turned back.

As the *Golden Hind* steered a course up the west coast of the continent, the fair weather they enjoyed was interpreted by Drake as a token of Divine approval for their voyage on state affairs—which the Spanish continued to refer to as piracy. Evidence seems to lean toward the Spanish interpretation, since the Englishmen took many rich prizes from peaceful towns and ships before they reached the coast of Costa Rica and anchored in the secluded mouth of a creek.

Drake may not have had Divine sponsorship, but his luck was certainly riding high. The very next day he captured a little frigate that made the mistake of passing the mouth of the creek. On board were two China trade pilots, complete with their charts and sailing directions for the navigation of the Pacific. Gales blew the *Golden Hind* northward along the coast of California to San Francisco. The report of the first Englishmen to sail the Pacific would not be acceptable today to the California Chamber of Commerce. It is recorded that the land was barren, the trees without leaves, and "the birds dared not leave their nests till the eggs were hatched."

Late July found the English leaving the west coast of America and pushing out into the open Pacific. They touched at several small islands and finally reached the Philippines. In the Celebes Sea a roaring monsoon drove the *Golden Hind* on a shoal. The ship seemed certain of disaster, but the admiral's luck held, and she finally slipped off into the deep water.

After touching at many islands along the coast of Asia, Drake laid his course for the Cape of Good Hope and home. It was near the end of September, 1580, when the *Golden Hind* dropped anchor once again in Plymouth harbor. The voyage of the first Englishmen to circumnavigate the globe had taken three years.

It was late in the eighteenth century before the tiny east coast English seaport of Whitby garnered any recognition. And it took the navigational, diplomatic and medicinal skills of Captain James Cook, in a journey half way 'round the world to what were then the Sandwich Islands and are today America's fiftieth state, to achieve this.

Cook served his early apprentice years with a firm of shipowners in Whitby, joining the Royal Navy in 1755. Twelve years later, as a Lieutenant in command of the *Endeavour*, he circumnavigated the globe and carried out extensive explorations of the coast lines of both Australia and New Zealand.

In the years which followed, Cook conducted exploratory voyages throughout the vast areas of the South Pacific, varying his seamanship with astute practices of other sciences. His successful struggles against the twin threats of scurvy and fever contributed much to modern hygienic practices, and it was on Tahiti that he set up an observatory, in 1769, to view "the passage of the Planet Venus over the disc of the Sun."

His achievements in diversified fields were so great and so universally respected, that the historian Fiske reports:

> When Franklin was in Paris as representative of the United States he was empowered to issue Letters of Marque against the English, but in doing so, inserted an instruction that if any of the holders should fall in with vessels commanded by Captain Cook, he was to be shown every respect and be permitted to pass unattacked on account of the benefits he had conferred on mankind through his important discoveries.

Despite his proclivities for science, the Captain had a continuing interest in food. A good part of his interest was brought about by the fact that as a good commander, he had to provision his ships. But he also took a delight in new food discoveries, providing they were adapted to his British tastes. On one occasion he recorded his observations on the making of a pudding:

Of Breadfruit, Ripe Plantains, Taro, and Palm or Pandanus nuts, each rasped down, scraped, or beat up fine and baked by itself; a quantity of juice expressed from Cocoanut Kernels was put into a large tray or wooden vessel, amongst it the other articles piping hot, as they were taken out of the oven, and a few hot stones just to keep the whole simmering.

Captain Cook was so taken with this concoction that he "seldom or never dined without one" when he could get it. He even went so far as to say, "we can make few in England that equal it."

All through his famous journals, there are references to the exchange of gifts. Cook reports that he was invited to the house of a Tahitian Chieftain to observe the dressing of two girls in gifts of cloth. One end of each piece of cloth was held up over the heads of the girls:

whilst the remainder was wrapped around them under the armpits; then the upper ends were let fall and hung down in folds to the ground over the other and looked something like a circular hooped petticoat. Afterward round the outside of all were wrapped several pieces of different colored cloth, which considerably increased the size, so that the whole was not less than five or six yards in circuit and was as much as the poor girls could support. To each was hung two "Teames" or breast plates by way of enriching the whole. Thus equipped they were conducted on board ship together with several hogs and a quantity of fruit as a present from Otoo's Father to me.

On his third voyage, he planned to cruise into the Arctic, and the necessity for preserving the expedition's store of spirits against the rigors of the North was quite apparent. While they were still at Tahiti, Cook called together the crew of his flagship, and suggested that they might discontinue the issue of grog, since the supply of cocoanuts was so plentiful, and provided such an excellent drink. The exception to this ban was to be Saturday night, "when they (the crew) had full allowance to drink to their female friends in England, lest amongst the pretty girls of Otaheite they should be wholly forgotten."

The cultural gap between the customs of life in England and the "Society Islands," is dramatized in a ceremony Cook attended during his last visit there.

Two of the islands were preparing for war upon each other. One of the chieftains sent word to Cook that he had killed a man of his own island as a sacrifice to his gods, hoping that the sacrifice would evoke divine assistance. Cook was invited to attend the ceremonies of the sacrifice. He took the opportunity to study the customs of the natives.

When the chieftain asked if such ceremonies were practiced in England, Cook told him that if the highest chief in all of England ever killed one man, he would be hanged. This so disturbed the native chieftain that he shouted at the Englishman in protest:

"Vile! Vile!"

Cook's comment summed up the situation with commendable objectivity. He said, ". . . we left him with as great a contempt for our customs as we could possibly have for theirs."

Captain Cook and other Europeans who came to the South Pacific added many things to the simple cultures they found. One innovation that is said to have aroused great curiosity among the Polynesians for a short while was horseback riding. When the Polynesians were given horses as a gift, they were puzzled about the use that could be made of them. So when Cook and his men rode the horses about the islands, great crowds gathered to watch them. Cook said he thought the islanders were more impressed by the art of horseback riding than anything else the British did.

According to the account of at least one historian, the Polynesians lost interest in their horses very quickly. Half-a-century later, when a horse was brought to one of the islands as a gift, the people were frightened by the "man-carrying-pig."

PART 6

Unsung Heroes
of the Seaports

A BRISK wind was blowing off the water on the eighth day of April, 1845. At Blackwall Shipyard in London Port, just up the river from the East India docks, the morning sun glinted on the tall poles of a rugged frigate, newly launched. She was a full-rigged ship, 175 feet long, with two decks and a spar deck with a square stern. The name lettered on bow and stern was *Alfred*.

Shipbuilder George Green, her constructor, walked slowly up and down the dock, peering with a knowing eye at every detail of her

makeup. A powerful man, despite his seventy-one years, broad of shoulder, keen of vision, Green had an enormous pride in this, his latest creation. Many times in his thirty-odd years of shipbuilding he had sent ships of his own design from the Blackwall ways to all parts of the world. The *Alfred* he considered his masterpiece.

A holiday crowd has gathered around the docks. Sir Gerald Ryan, impressive chief justice of Bengal (for this ship is destined for the East India trade) presides at the ceremony of commissioning. A weathered old seaman, Captain Alexander Henning, who is to command the *Alfred*, talks quietly with a prospective shareholder from one of the ship insurance companies.

Finally George Green completes his inspection, satisfied that all is shipshape. He gives the word for the commissioning ceremony to begin and climbs to the platform; he graciously pays his homage to the Chief Justice and his lady and takes his seat.

But the oratory passed easily over his head. Green was thinking back—to the day he first came to Blackwell yard, a penniless apprentice—sixty-three years ago!

The *Alfred* was originally laid down for the British Admiralty—a thirty-six gun frigate. But changes in ship design were afoot. To the Admiralty powers it looked as though the revolutionary paddle-wheel frigate might soon make ordinary sailing ships obsolete—especially warships. The Admiralty, therefore, had taken a second thought and decided to renegotiate its contract.

"If you don't want this ship," shipbuilder Green said, "we'll buy her." And the firm agreed.

The most powerful force in the development of ships has always been the changing demands of new hazardous trade routes and commercial cargoes. The earlier East Indiamen, for example, were merchant ships; but because they had to defend themselves against pirates and privateers of other nations, they went armed and were actually men-of-war, privately owned. Thus speed was highly important to them. So was armament. The Dutch and Portuguese, of course, took no kindly view of the invasion of their rich colonial area by these enterprising British. Hardly a passage was made by any ship without the exchange of courtesies in the form of round shots. That is why these East Indiamen won fame for their fighting capacity as well as for their cargo-carrying abilities.

Speed, on the other hand, was the prime quality of the West Indiamen built in the Port of London for trade with the new world. They were constructed to carry special cargoes—mainly fruit and slaves. The earlier West Indiamen were only 500 tons. They sailed in convoy, often accompanied by men-of-war for protection. And if the owner could make a fair profit out of a cargo carried on a ship so small, he was satisfied.

Yet another ship type was being developed in London for the

North Atlantic trade—the packet. The first packets were English—built for the Boston Importing Company to establish a regular service between London, Liverpool and Boston. That was in 1805.

The War of 1812, of course, interrupted the budding trade of the American- and British-built packets between the two countries. America's Black Ball Line and Swallowtail Line started a London-New York service soon after the war was over. The *Corinthian*, the *Brighton*, the *Columbian*, the *Cortez*, all flying the Red and White Swallowtail of their owners, soon proved their value as moneymakers in the New York trade.

The famous American Clipper ships reached the peak of their beauty and speed in the illicit opium trade, though they had a far more prosaic origin. In 1839 the little British clipper schooner *Scottish Maid* slid down the ways in Aberdeen, Scotland. She was designed by Alexander Hall to compete with the several little British-built paddle-wheel ships in the coastal trade. She had beautiful lines and was schooner rigged. When she sailed up the Thames, London shouted vociferous welcome. Soon her sister-ships headed to the Mediterranean for business. Fast little sailing vessels, they were of only 150 tons burden. Their high reputation lay in their remarkable ability to bring their cargoes undamaged through rough weather.

The British shipbuilders, as a whole, didn't take kindly to the clipper design until the first American clipper appeared in 1832. She was the famous *Ann McKim* built in Baltimore—thus the term "Baltimore Clipper." So fast and successful was she in the China run, even though her cargo capacity was small, that the British hurried to their own drawing boards to make improvements on this clipper design.

Many clippers were designed for special cargoes: fruit, opium, and similar "express" items. But the threat of steam was becoming increasingly evident. With its full development and emergence, the great romantic days of sailing came to an end.

In one sense, the unsung heroes of the seaports were the George Greens, the Alexander Halls and such men as Hercules Linton, designer and builder of the *Cutty Sark*, most famous of all the clipper ships. Even the smuggling, tax-evading citizens of Palos must be included in this category, for without their valiant efforts, Columbus would never have reached the New World.

The story of seaports and people is largely the history of navigators and adventurers, of heroes and rogues, of monarchs and galley slaves, of romantics and raiders. Yet, it is also the story of the designers and builders who worked, without history's recognition, to design and construct the finest, most seaworthy vessels that the knowledge and technology of their day would permit.

Without the dedication and skill of these men there would have been no fame for the Magellans, the Maria-Carolinas, the da Gamas, or even for the Simon von Utrechts! Alexander the Great, Henry of Portugal, Captain Cook—all owe much of their achievement to the unknowns who planned their ships and the gangs of little men who cut and hewed and curved and fitted the planks that made their craft competent to ride out the turbulance of the world's untracked sea lanes.

Even so great a monarch as the effete and profligate Charles II owes some part of his royal opulence to the Venetian shipbuilders who preceded him in history by some five hundred years! For, in the midst of his seventeenth century reign, this Stuart King found himself deep in debt to several gentlemen of Venice who had loaned him large sums of money.

He could pay neither in goods nor in cash. So, profiting from news that had been borne to England long since in some Venetian-built ship, he gave his creditors the same right, in London, that an earlier Doge had granted to Nicola Barattiere back in the year 1127.

Between two columns under the Arch of Covent Gardens, the Venetian merchants, by royal permission, set up gaming tables!

Trade, romance, adventure, struggles for political and personal power—the world has seen all of these from its earliest days. Through its seaports and the people who made history from them, the world and its civilization have gained much knowledge. What progress mankind has so far witnessed could not have been achieved had it not been for the thousands of years of continual, dogged seafaring by brave and daring men and women, whose travels resulted in interchange of cultures, merchandise and ideas.

PERSONAL POSTSCRIPT

Writing this volume of European and Near Eastern seaports has given me a vast satisfaction. It has carried me back in spirit to the seaports themselves, bringing still more vividly to mind the places, sights, sounds, and smells that characterize each, and the people—especially the friends I have made in many of them. There is, for example, the Countess Ethel de Gramedo, now living in Paris, at whose home I have spent happy hours on various visits; and the Duchesse de Prezenzano of Naples, whose villa is in that always fascinating seaport.

High up also on my list of friends, I would put the name of the late Viscount Waverly, for many years head of the Port of London Authority. I met Lord and Lady Waverly on an Italian holiday in 1954. It was he who first wakened my interest in that great British seaport, whose activities so influenced American history.

THE VIEW FROM A BRIDGE

Less than six months have passed, as I write this page, since I stood on Tower Bridge over the Thames in London and looked down on the activities of London Pool: a lively stretch of river where, I believe, more ships and boats of a greater variety assemble at any day's end than anywhere in the world—certainly in any port that I have ever visited.

The dusk of an early spring day was weaving its veil over the city, softening the sharp outlines of one or two Nazi-bombed buildings, the jagged edges of many new structures going up to replace the wreckage of war; reducing to a single soft and soothing monotone the prevailing grime-touched grey-and-white of the ancient town.

Down there below me in the river, the first lights flashed on to glimmer on some colliers toiling in to dock. Tugs screamed their salutations to another day's work done as they cut loose from convoys of barges they had been towing, and now left anchored on the stream's bosom. A couple of Thames excursion steamers, slender and sharp of prow, came paddling smoothly by, bringing crowds from a day-long jaunt. Several old sailing ships—now historic sights to be seen by visiting tourists for a modest fee—lay tied up not many blocks away.

Cargo vessels—some pot-bellied and murky with the salt and the dirt of long service, others new and of fine lines—lay at their berths identified by known houseflags and funnel markings. A few moderate sized passenger liners. A conglomerate fleet of diversified small craft—chugging, whoofing, blaring or silent. Such is London Pool at dusk.

Englishmen claim that the Port of London, of which the Pool is only a small segment, is the world's largest. Most likely they're right. Indubitably so if one measures the port in its area of extent. The Port of London Authority covers a sixty-five-mile stretch. It reaches all the way down to Gravesend. From an airplane you can see the full length of the port on a clear day and beyond, to Tilbury, and the series of small "lakes" opening off the main stem of the parent river.

Standing there, on the Bridge and calling to mind the close connection between what has happened in this port during the last four centuries and our own United States, I could not but remember that a still stronger tie has been forged between the two countries since I started writing this book, in collaboration with Garnett Eskew, more than a year ago.

For since then, the St. Lawrence Seaway has been completed. The maritime interdependence between the two great English-speaking nations has been further cemented by the visit of Queen Elizabeth to the Seaway opening ceremonies where she, with President Eisenhower, once again emphasized and strengthened our sea alliance.

May this happy event prove one more step in building further goodwill not only between the United States and the British Commonwealth of Nations, but between all other nations of the free world whose ships will now be sailing deep into North America, thereby strengthening the kinship of the Family of Man.

BIBLIOGRAPHY

ADAMS, JAMES TRUSLOW, *Building the British Empire.*
    New York-London, C. Scribner's Sons, 1938.
ADAMS, WM. H. D., *English Heroes in the Reign of Queen Elizabeth.*
    Edinburgh, W. P. Nimmo, Hay & Mitchell, 1902.
ANDERSON, SVEN A., *Vikings.* New York, Columbia University Press, 1936.
ANTHONY, IRVING, *Down to the Sea in Ships.*
    Philadelphia, Penn. Publishing Co., 1924.
ANTHONY, IRVING, *Voyagers Unafraid.*
    Philadelphia, Macrae Smith Co., 1930.
BARNOUW, A. J., *The Making of Modern Holland.*
    London, Geo. Allen & Unwin Ltd., 1948.
BARNOUW, A. J., *Pageant of Netherlands History.*
    New York, Longmans Green & Co., 1952.
BEAZLEY, CHAS. R., *Prince Henry the Navigator.*
    London-New York, G. P. Putnam's Sons, 1895.
BELL, ALAN, *Port of London.* London, Port of London Authority, 1934.
BOURNE, H. R., *Romance of Trade.*
    New York-London, Cassell, Petter & Galpin, 1871.
BOWEN, FRANK C., *Conquest of the Sea.*
    New York, R. M. McBride & Co., 1940.
BOWEN, FRANK C., *Port of London.* London, Dryden Periodicals, 1949.
BOYESEN, HJALMAR H., *Story of Norway.*
    London-New York, G. P. Putnam's Sons, 1886.
BROGGER, ANTON W., *The Viking Ships.* London, Edw. Stanford Ltd., 1953.
COGGESHALL, GEO., *Historical Sketch of Commerce.*
    New York, G. P. Putnam, 1860.
CORBETT, J., *Drake and the Tudor Navy.*
    New York-London, Longman's Green, 1898.
CORBETT, J., *England and the Mediterranean.*
    New York, Geo. H. Doran & Co., 1917.
CORREA, GASPAR, *The Three Voyages of Vasco da Gama.*
    London, Hakluyt Society, 1869.
DAY, CLIVE, *A History of Commerce.* New York, Longman's-Green, 1938.
GOSSE, PHILIP, *Sir John Hawkins.*
    London, John Lane (The Bodley Head Press, Ltd.), 1930.
HUMPHERENS, HENRY, *Company of the Waterman of the Thames.*
    London, S. Prentice, 1874–1886.
INGLETON, GEOFFREY C., *Explorations of Capt. James Cook.*
    New York, Heritage Press, 1958.
JACKSON, JOHN H., *Finland.* New York, The Macmillan Co., 1940.

Bibliography

Keilhau, Wilhelm C., *Norway in World History*.
London, Macdonald & Co., 1944.
Kubly, H., *American in Italy*. New York, Simon & Schuster, 1955.
Nunn, Geo. E., *Magellan's Route in the Pacific*.
New York, American Geographical Society, 1934.
Prance, Cyril R., *Knights of the Sea*. London, Quality Press, 1938.
Riemens, Hendrik, *The Netherlands*. New York, Eagle Books, 1944.
Tarbox, Increase Niles, *Tyre & Alexandria*.
Boston, Sabbath School Society, 1865.
Van Cleef, Eugene, *Trade Centers & Trade Routes*.
New York-London, D. Appleton-Century Co. Inc., 1937.
Walling, Robt. A. J., *A Sea-Dog of Devon*.
New York, John Lane Co., 1907.
Williamson, James Alex., *Sir John Hawkins*.
Oxford, Clarendon Press, 1927.
Wilson, King, *Chronicles of 3 Free Cities*. New York, E. P. Dutton, 1914.
Zimmern, Helen, *The Hansea Towns*.
New York, G. P. Putnam's Sons, 1889.

INDEX